Blues & Rock
HARMONICA

By Glenn Weiser

This book is dedicated to the memory of Paul Butterfield

Special thanks go to Larry Rappoport, who took the photographs in this book, to Linda Baker, who typed the manuscript, to Margie Rosenkranz, who edited the text, and Mark King, who contributed to the discography. Any correspondence regarding this work may be addressed to me at: Box 2551 ESP, Albany, NY 12220

Cover Art by Eddie Young
Calligraphy by George Ports
Layout and Production by Ron Middlebrook

ISBN   0-931759-41-2
SAN   683-8022

lucky

Contents

INTRODUCTION

My introduction to blues harp took place in the summer of 1968 when I was 16. It consisted of just one informal lesson. The place was the Boston common, which was at the time the hub of the local psychedelic subculture. It was a gathering place for musicians, poets, artists, radicals, philosophers, professors, priests, winos, dealers, bikers, teeny boppers, tourists just there looking at all the wierdness and many other people, including myself-a sort of casual observer.

I just happened to be carrying a harmonica and one day I met a musician (whose name I never learned) amid the throng of the Common's long-haired habitues. He was wearing sunglasses and a denim jacket and said he could play both the guitar and the harmonica. I asked him to show me how to play the harp, which I had been fooling around with but as yet could make no sense of. He began by explaining that blues riffs were centered around the draw notes. We sat down in the dust, he demonstrated a bit, and then played some blues on his guitar while I tried to solo. After a while he commented that I had "come out with some good lines," and stood up and drifted off into the crowd. I never saw him again.

After that I jammed with other musicians at every chance. Opportunities were abundant as everybody, it seemed, could play a bit of guitar. By the end of the summer I was getting somewhere with it, although already being a guitar player admittedly helped.

Late in August I said good-bye to the flower children and returned home to New Jersey where I kept on blowing harp. The harmonica wound up in my pocket wherever I went and there was plenty of time to practice. Eventually, I got to be a fairly good harp player.

I also progressed on the guitar as well as other instruments, and over the course of time, carved out a niche for myself as an instrumental music instructor. Of all the musical skills I possessed and was able to teach, improvisation was the most intangible. It resisted analysis, forcing me to think hard about a workable system of explaining it. After pulling enough mental muscles, I came up with the three-stage system detailed in Chapter 8, which is basically the core of this book.

This is, by the way, my second book on the harmonica (The first, **FIDDLE TUNES FOR HARMONICA,** is a collection of over 100 Irish, New England, Southern and even a few original tunes arranged for harmonica and accompaniment). This book, written at the invitation of Ron Middlebrook of CENTERSTREAM Publications, is designed to take a beginner on the instrument to an advanced understanding of playing technique and the principles of improvisation. It can either be enjoyed for its riffs and solos or studied seriously as a blues harp textbook. The several exercises contained in the book are designed to help you learn the various skills that should be possessed by any good harp player.

Based on the premise that the harmonica is as much of a musical instrument as any other despite its low cost, this book covers some aspects of music theory that are relevant to blues and rock improvisation. In these pages you will find precise explanations of scales, modes, chords and other essential elements of music. If you take the time to absorb the information contained in this volume and work at the exercises, you will be playing from a vantage point far superior to the hit-and-miss approach of playing by ear. To sum it up: the more you know, the more you can do. Learn the contents of this book and you will be able to master blues and rock harmonica.

It is not necessary to know how to read music in order to use this book. How to read rhythms is discussed in Chapter 3, and each note in the riffs and solos has the appropriate hole number below it. All you have to do is follow the rhythms, reading the hole numbers. Explanations of scales, chords and improvisation are all given in terms of the steps of the scale rather than by note names, and therefore do not depend on written music.

Even though the bulk of the book is devoted to the blues, it is important to understand that rock grew out of the blues. If you can play blues harp, you can play rock. The chords used in rock songs vary as opposed to the set pattern of the blues, but the riffs are basically the same. How to adapt blues harp to rock chord changes is explained in Chapter 11.

This book comes with a tape cassette on which I have recorded the riffs and solos plus demonstrations of the various playing techniques. The tape (on which a A-scale harp is used), concludes with a blues jam in G that you play along with.

So-take out your harp, open up to Chapter 1 and get ready to wail!

Yours Bluely,
Glenn Weiser

Larry Rappoport

Glenn   Weiser

CHAPTER ONE

-About The Harmonica-

The story of the harmonica begins with the Chinese Emperor Nyn-Kwya, who in 3000 B. C. invented a free-reed instrument called the "sheng' (sublime voice) which is considered the forerunner of the modern harmonica.

The Sheng was brought to Europe in the 18th Century, where the idea of the free-reed principle was used in the creation of the reed organ, the accordian, the concertina, the saxophone, and the harmonica.

The modern harmonica was invented in 1821 by a German clockmaker named Christian Buschman who put fifteen pitch pipes together to create an odd little instrument. At first harmonicas were produced by clockmakers as a sideline, but in 1857 Matthias Hohner decided to manufacture them on a large scale and went into production in Trossingen, Germany.

The harmonica spread all over Germany, and with the mass emigration of Germans in the latter half of the nineteenth century, all over the world. By the time of the American Civil War, the harmonica was well established in the United States and many soldiers on both sides played them. At first the repertory in this country for harmonica consisted of folksongs, fiddle tunes, marches, hymns and the like, but somewhere along the way it was taken up by the black man and its previously unrealized potential as a blues instrument came to light.

The origins of blues harp in the South remain obscure in spite of all the musicological research that has been done in the area of the blues. Probably the discovery that the notes could be lowered in pitch by changing the pressure exerted on reeds was an accidental one, but nonetheless the 'blue" notes of the African vocal scale and the moans and cries of the field holler had been successfully reproduced on a new instrument. By the 1920's, blues harp was a common sound in the South. (Sonny Terry's playing represents the best of the rural styles).

After World War ll there was a large shifting of the black population from the rural south to the urban north, especially Chicago. Starting from the late thirties, four giants of blues harmonica recorded and performed in Chicago: Sonny Boy Willianson, Little Walter Jacobs, Big Walter Horton and Rice (Sonny Boy Williamson II) Miller (see discography).

Together these men created the sound of the Chicago-style blues harmonica with its various moods and voice-like sounds, ranging from eerie howls and raucous yells to whispers and sighs. It was a compelling sound, demanding and getting instant attention.

A second generation of harpmen, consisting of Junior Wells, James Cotton, Paul Butterfield, Charlie Musselwhite and others, learned the art directly from the older masters (except for Sonny Boy I, who was murdered in 1948). Paul Butterfield (1941-1987) was undoubtedly the greatest of this second generation, and did much to popularize the harmonica as a blues and rock instrument.

The advent of rock n' roll in the mid-fifties gave the blues themselves the blues. Sales of blues records dropped, many performers had to seek other livelihoods and even Muddy Waters (whose bands always featured a harmonica player) found that audiences were unreceptive to slow blues in the nightclubs of Chicago.

Meanwhile, the blues were being discovered in Europe, especially England, where young guitarists with names like Clapton, Beck, and Page were wearing holes in their records figuring out the riffs of B. B. King, Albert King, and other American black blues guitarists. The blues-based British rock invasion of the late sixties repopularized the blues, but now the audiences were young whites rather than blacks, who had moved on to R & B, soul, and jazz. Unfortunately, the creators of the style got none of the credit until 1964, when The Rolling Stones appeared on the TV show "Shindig" along with blues legend Howlin' Wolf (The Stones got Wolf on the show by refusing to play without him).

Mick Jagger, John Lennon, Neil Young, Bob Dylan, Al Wilson of Canned Heat, Pig Pen of the Grateful Dead and other famous sixties musicians all played the harmonica and helped establish it as a rock as well as a blues instrument. With the recent (late 80's) resurgence of interest in the blues, the fate of the blues harp playing seems secure indeed.

The harmonica itself consists of a wood or plastic body called a comb, two brass reed plates, and two nickel covers. The diatonic harmonica with which we are concerned (there are other types such as the chromatic, octave tuned and even a minor key model, but these are not usually used for the blues) has ten holes, each hole provides one of two different notes, depending on whether you are exhaling (called "blowing") or inhaling (called "drawing") . The 20 notes available on the harmonica cover a range of three octaves and are arranged in such a way that only the middle octave contains a complete scale. The lower octave lacks the fourth and seventh steps of the scale (the harmonica is designed this way in order to have the tonic and dominant chords in the lower register), and the upper octave lacks the seventh step of the scale.

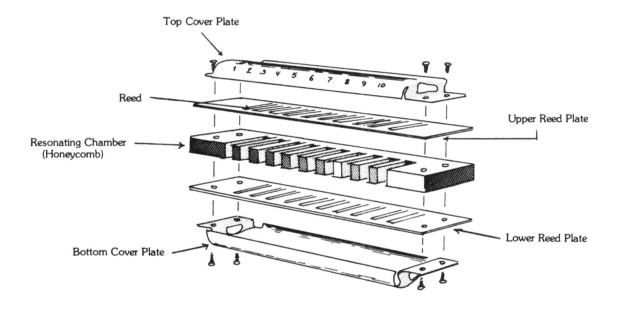

Most diatonic harmonicas are made by the Hohner Company, and one can choose from among the Marine Band, the Special 20, the Golden Melody and the Blues Harp. The Special 20 and Golden Melody have plastic combs while the Marine Band andthe Blues Harp have wooden combs, I recommend the Marine Band, although the Silvertone Model by the Huang Company the Lee Oskar harmonicas are very good too. Lower pitched harmonicas, being either the G, A, or C scales, are a little easier to learn on.

When you buy a harmonica, play softly for the first few days. This will help break it in. I also advise against soaking the harmonica in water, beer, gin, etc. Although this will break in the harmonica more quickly and increase the volume as well, it will also drastically decrease the life-span of the instrument. The best thing to do is just allow the harmonica to break in gradually and naturally. You will get more for your money. You should also keep the harmonica in its case when you are not playing it, because if a small particle of dirt or even a hair gets stuck in a reed, it can prevent a note from sounding. If this does happen, try using a pin to dislodge whatever is stuck.

Eventually, you will need a collection of harmonicas in order to be able to play with other musicans. Guitar players usually play in the keys of A, C, D, E, G, or F, so I always have at least a half-dozen harps with me if I am on my way to a club date or jam session. That way, I can play on just about any tune.

CHAPTER TWO

-GETTING STARTED-

The first aspect of playing technique is how to hold the harmonica. Lets start by first placing the harmonica in between the thumb and index finger of the left hand with the numbers facing up as shown in Figure I.

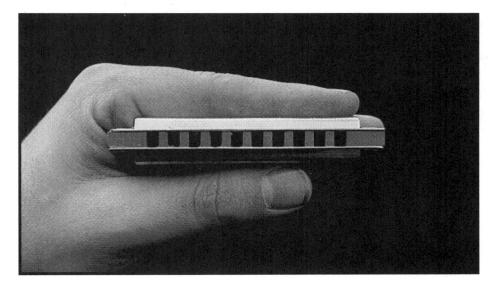

Figure 1

Next, bend your right hand back from your wrist and diagonally cover it with your left hand in such a way that the right index finger curls around the end of the left ring finger. The heels of the two palms should stay together. This cupping of the hands will enclose a pocket of air which can be rapidly or slowly opened and resealed by fluttering the right hand back from the wrist while the left hand remains steady. The quavering tone produced by this technique is called the **tremelo** and the configuration of the hands just described is therefore known as the tremelo position. (Figures 2 and 2a).

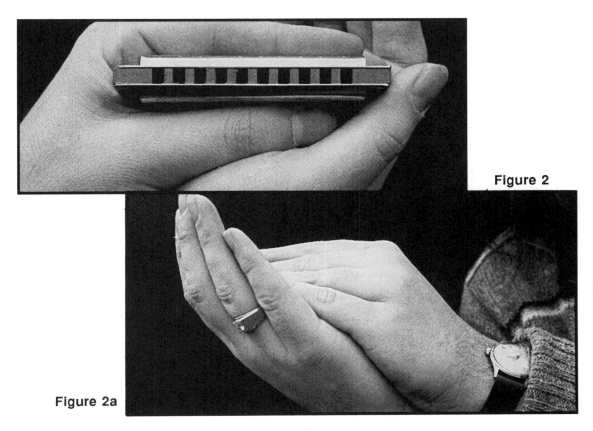

Figure 2

Figure 2a

The tremelo is usually more effective on long notes than shorter notes. The speed of the tremelo can also be varied by how fast you move the right hand.

After you have learned how to hold the harmonica, the next step is to learn how to properly blow and draw notes. Your lips should be curled out like a fish, and relaxed. Place the harmonica on the inside of your lips and try blowing a few notes in the lower reeds (you should be breathing from your diaphram). Then try drawing a few notes. There should be a slight tension in the sides of the mouth as you do this and your tongue should be on the bottom of your mouth. Your throat should be open, teeth slightly apart.

Your goal is to eventually be able to play one note at a time, with your lips blocking off the other reeds. This is by no means easy in the beginning, so at first, the best thing to do is to play riffs involving two or three notes at the same time. Remember, just breath gently. You do not need a lot of force to produce a tone. Next, try playing the first, second and third draw reeds together.

It will be written like this in the beginning:
```
3
2
1
```

Circled numbers will be used to indicate draw reeds ➡ ④

Uncircled numbers will indicate blow reeds. ➡ 4

The vertical line above the chord (three notes together make up a chord) indicates that the chord last for one beat. If you want to tap your foot, which will help to develop a good sense of time, each chord will last for one tap of the foot. Playing with a metronome, by the way, is also helpful.

Let's try a few basic riffs.

```
      /  /  /  /        /  /  /  /           /  /  /  /
     |3| 4 |4| 4       |4| 5 |5| 5          |2| 2 ① 2
  1) |2| 3 |3| 3    2) |3| 4 |4| 4       3) |1| 1    1
     |1| 2 |2| 2       |2| 3 |3| 3
     tap tap tap tap   tap tap tap tap      tap tap tap tap
```

Riffs 1 & 2 are both made up of three-note chords. Riff 3 is different as it has two-note chords and a single note on the third beat. Because riff 3 takes place at the low end of the harmonica (that is, the left side where the low notes are), playing two notes instead of three and even the single note ① should not be that difficult.

When playing a chord, it is important to have the correct top note, which is the note highest in pitch. The top note of any chord functions as the melody note, with the others functioning as harmony notes. Check yourself to see if you are playing the right chord or single note by taking the harp out of your mouth and laying your index fingers flat over all the reeds except the desired reed or reeds. Then, with your fingers still blocking the reeds, lift the harmonica to your mouth and play the chord or single note. After that, resume the tremelo position and play. As you play these first few riffs, listen to the tone of the notes. Do they sound distorted? Is there a hissing sound? If there is, you might not be sealing off the harmonica correctly with your lips. No air should be escaping from the top or bottom of the harmonica. You may have to adjust the position of the harp a little to correct the sibilant tone that results from not maintaining a good seal. Eventually correct tone production will become easy, given enough practice.

After you have been practicing the first three riffs for a while, take riffs 1 and 2 and play them as two-note riffs instead of three-note riffs. That will be like this:

```
1a  |3|  4   |4|  4        2a |4|  5   |5|  5
    |2|  3   |3|  3           |3|  4   |4|  4
```

Here again, you can block off the other reeds with your index fingers to check yourself for accuracy.

The next step is to try to play these riffs as single note phrases using only the top notes of the chords. Lower your jaw, make sure your lips are relaxed and see if you can isolate a single note. Try 4-draw as a start or 3-blow.

Don't be surprised if you experience difficulty with this, as getting a clear single note is a common problem in the beginning. Most of the people I have taught have been able to single out notes within a month, so just have patience and make sure that you are correctly following these instructions.

Pucker your lips and form a hole higher that it is wide: that is, in the shape of an upright or vertical oval. It should look more like a zero (0) than an "o". If the oval is too wide, you will get more than one note. If this happens, lower you jaw and remember to maintain a slight tension in the corners of your mouth. If the oval is too narrow, you will not be allowing air to exit and enter through your lips. Try relaxing your lips. If your single notes hiss, either the harmonica is not on the inside of your lips or your lips are too tense.

Tensing up the muscles in your lips, especially the upper lip, as well as the muscles in your jaw, will also prevent correct tone production. Your jaw should hang in a relaxed fashion. Muscular tension is also a common reaction to the initial frustration that can occur when you are unable to get a clear single note. Remember that any real skill is only learned with time and effort. Keep trying and you will get it!

Once you succeed in getting a clear single note the next two things are: to learn to change from a draw to a blow note on the same reed, and to move from a draw note to a neigboring draw note or from a blow note to a neighboring blow note. When you change from draw to blow (or vice versa), be sure to maintain the correct lip position without puffing out your cheeks or blowing too hard. When going in between neighboring notes, move the harmonica rather than your head and keep both lips on the harp.

Also, it is not necessary to take air into your lungs whenever you play a draw note. Basically, you are blowing and drawing with the air in your mouth as you maintain a pattern of slow, deep respiration, with part of the breathing occuring through the nose. All of this becomes natural with practice. Try these simple riffs:

```
        /    /    /    /  |   /    /    /    /
4)     ④   3   ②   2  |  ①   2   ②   3

         /    /    /    /  |   /    /    /    /
5)     ③   4   ④   5  |  ⑤   5   ④   ③

         /    /    /    /  |
6)     ②   ③   ④   5  |

         /    /    /    /  |   /    /    /    /
7)     ②   ③   3   2  |  ②   ①   ②   3

         /    /    /    /  |   /    /    /    /
8)     6   5   ⑤   5  |  ④   4   ③   3
```

One last hint--if ③ does not sound good, try making sure that you are breathing through your noes a well as your mouth. ③ and also ② can be tricky at first.

Sonny Terry

CHAPTER THREE

-MUSIC NOTATION-

In order to play the riffs and solos in this book, you will need to know something about music notation. Because the hole numbers below each note tell you which note to play, being able to read the rhythms will be far more important than being able to read the pitches (the positions of the notes in the staff).

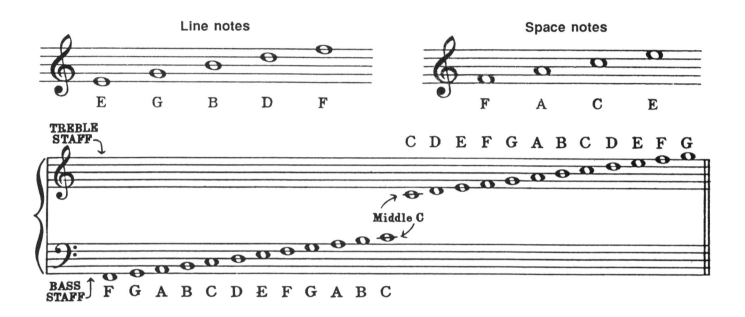

The staff (above) consists of five lines and four spaces. Notes will appear either on the lines or in the spaces. The names of the lines, going up, are: E, G, B, D and F. The names of the spaces are F, A, C and E.

The staff can be extended either upwards or downwards by the use of ledger lines.

The symbol at the beginning of the staff is the G clef signature (which designates the second line as G), also called treble clef.

This chapter is not intended to be a complete course in reading music, but rather a guide to interpreting the rhythms you will encounter in the riffs and solos. Reading music on the harmonica is somewhat impractical for the reason that every time you play a different scale harmonica, the notes, if they were written out, would change position in the staff. This is why the hole numbers are always provided in harmonica music.

We will need at least one key in order to notate music, so the examples will be written in the key of F. This is indicated by the symbol ♭ (which is a flat sign) placed on the line B just to the right of the clef signature. One flat is the key signature of F, so the examples will therefore be written for the F scale harmonica. For technical reasons, F is a good key in which to write even though the F scale harmonica is high-pitched. Any scale harmonica can be used to play the music in this book, however.

HERE IS A LISTING OF THE NOTES ON THE F SCALE HARMONICA.

TABLE 1

hole	1	2	3	4	5	6	7	8	9	10
blow (out)	F	A	C	F	A	C	F	A	C	F
draw (in)	G	C	E	G	Bb	D	E	G	Bb	D

TABLE 1a

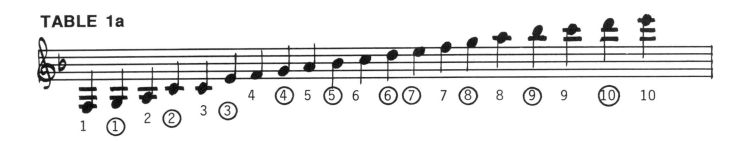

In Example 1 there are several different kinds of notes: quarter notes in the first measure, half notes in the second measure, and a whole note in the third measure (the staff is divided into measures by the vertical lines which are called the bar lines). The time signature at the beginning indicates that there are four beats to the measure.

The quarter note receives one beat.
The half note receives two beats.
The whole note receives four beats.
A beat is also referred to as a count.

The numbers above the notes show how Example 1 is counted out. As you begin to learn to read the rhythms, tap your foot on each count, that is, four times per measure. Measures #4-6 illustrate combinations of half notes and quarter notes.

In the last two measures, you will see a dotted half note (𝅗𝅥.). A dot can be placed after any type of note and extends its time value by half. Therefore, a dotted half note would be three counts long. A dotted quarter note would be a count and a half, etc.

Example 1

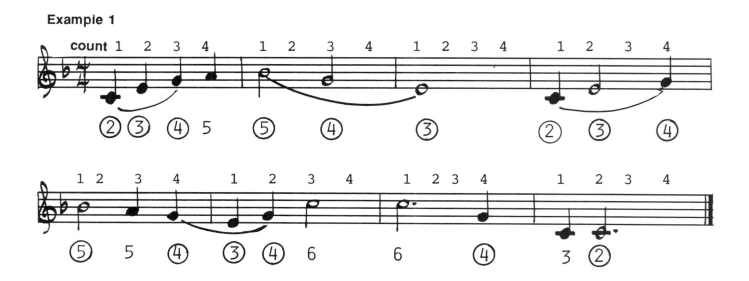

●**BREATH INDICATIONS**--The curved lines below the first three notes in measures #1 and 4, and below the first two notes in measure #6 are breath indications, also called **slur** marks. This means that these notes are to be played with the same breath, which is the way that two or more neighboring in or out reeds will usually be played.

As well as the whole, half and quarter notes, we will also be playing eighth notes, triplets, "swing'" eighth notes, sixteenth notes, accidentals, rests and ties. Let's discuss them one at a time.

Example 2 illustrates eighth notes. When a quarter note is divided into two equal parts, the result is two eighth notes. If written together, the stems are connected by a horizontal line called a **beam**( ) If written separately, the stems are said to be **flagged** ( ). When you play any riff or solo containing eighth notes, count "and" after each beat. If you are tapping your foot, it should be up on the "ands".

Example 2

●**TONGUING**--When you play Example 2, you have to use a technique called tonguing whenever you play the second note in a pair of eighths. Tonguing is done by whispering the word "two" as you blow or draw a note. This is done whenever a note is repeated, to clarify the distinction between the two notes by stopping the flow of air. Tonguing is also done when going in between two draw reeds or two blow reeds that are not next to each other, and if the two notes are eighths, triplets or sixteenths.

Example 3 shows you how two or three notes would be written together. These are chords. Use tonguing on the repetition of each chord just as you would when repeating a single note.

Example 3

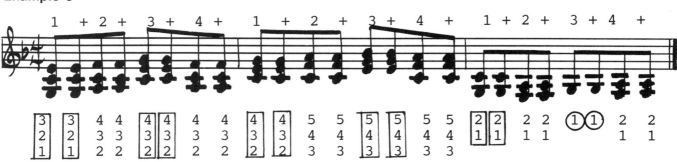

● **TRIPLETS**--Example 4 illustrates triplets, which is the division of a quarter note into three. Triplets are counted by saying. "ONE triplet, TWO triplet, THREE triplet, FOUR triplet."

You will notice that the first note in the example, ② or C, can also be played as 3-blow (sometimes it is more convenient to play this note as 3-out instead of 2-in).

Example 4

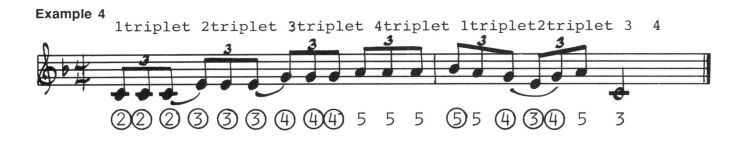

● **VIBRATO**--You can also use vibrato on the last note in example 4, which is done by constricting the muscles of the diaphram and throat as you blow the note. This will make the note, take on a warbling or quavering sound somewhat like a rapid tremelo and has a quality all of its own. This technique can also be used with the draw reeds (② with vibrato is a common sound in blues harp playing) and will liven up the longer notes. Vibrato is an important technique to master and is one of the marks of an accomplished Chicago-style harmonicist.

● **REST SIGNS**--A rest is a period of silence. Each type of note has a rest which corresponds to it:

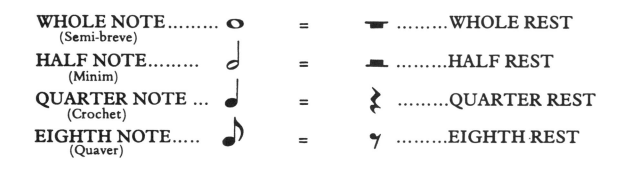

Example 5 shows a riff with rest.

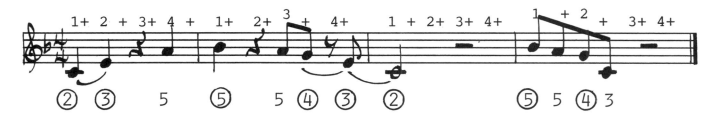

● **TIE**--A tie connects the time value of two notes of the same pitch. The second note is not played, but held. This is why you will not see a harmonica indication (a hole number) underneath the second note of a tie. Example 6 gives us a riff with ties.

Example 6

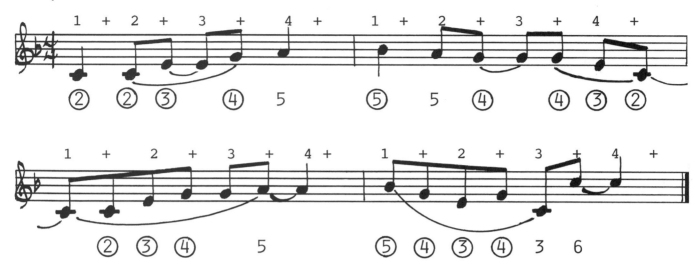

Do not get the ties confused with the breath indications. Remember, ties will always connect notes of the same pitch, and breath indications will always connect notes of different pitches. The use of ties, as we will see, can produce some very funky rhythms. When notes occuring off the beat are tied to those on the beat, it is called **syncopation** and is one of the most important characteristics of blues, jazz, rock and all other forms of music influenced by African rhythm.

● **"SWING EIGHTHS"**--are produced by tying the first two members of a triplet. This would look like this: ♪♪ . It could also be written like this: ♪ . Swing eighths are also written, although it is not really accurate, like this: ♫ Swing eighths are also used quite commonly with triplets. As an exercise, repeat examples 2, 3, 5 and 6 with swing eighths instead of even or "straight" eighths.

All of the riffs and solos in this book, unless otherwise indicated, will be played with swing eighths, which is a common rhythm in the blues. Example 7 shows how swing eighths are counted out.

Example 7

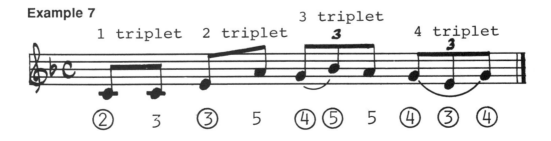

15

● **PICK-UP MEASURE & SIXTEENTH NOTES**--Example 8 shows two new things;
1) The pick-up measure, which is an incomplete measure preceding the first complete
measure, and sixteenth notes. 2). Sixteenth notes are usually heard in slow blues, especially
when a player wants to demonstrate his technical skill, and in this book only occur in the final
chapter. They are counted, "1 a & a, 2 a & a," etc.

Solo 1

This uses a walking (that is, steady quarter note rhythm) boogie-woogie pattern. Solo #2 is
virtually identical to Solo #1 except that is an octave higher, and has been included to get
you used to the upper reeds.

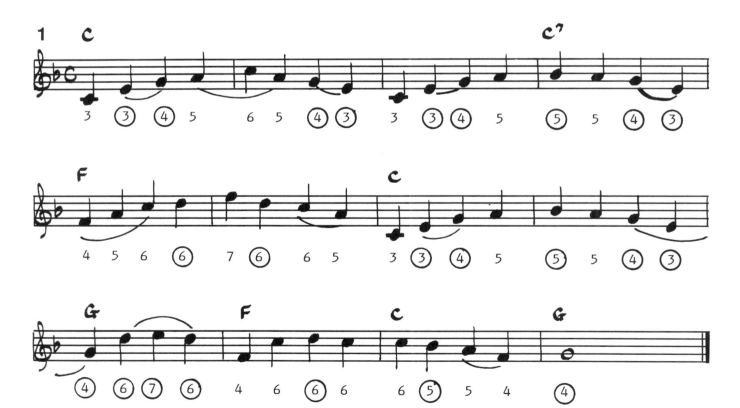

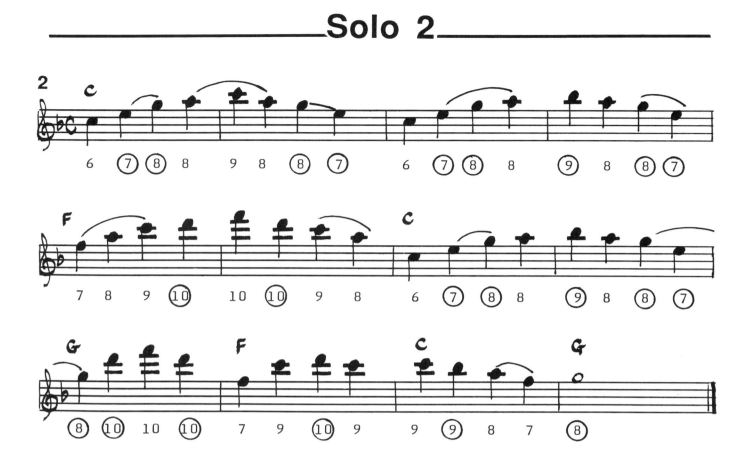

We have already mentioned the the flat sign (♭) in connection with the key signature. There is also the sharp sign (♯) and the natural (♮) sign. Sharps and flats are both known as **accidentals**. A flat sign lowers the pitch of a note by a half-step (this term will be further explained later) and a sharp sign raises the note by a half step. As for the <u>key signature</u>, the placement of the flat sign on the line B next to clef signature means that B will be read as B-flat throughout the piece, unless a natural sign appears before the note B. If a natural sign does appear, it restores B-flat to B-natural, either until the end of the measure or the appearance of another B-flat, whichever comes sooner. Similarly, if a sharp or flat sign appears before a note the note will be read as being either sharped or flatted until the end of the measure or the appearance of a natural sign in front of a subsequent note of the same pitch. Flats, sharps and naturals will not appear in the music until we get to note bending, and even then the harmonica indications will tell you exactly what to do.

INCREASE YOUR RHYTHM SKILLS

The first exercise involves taking the first two solos and repeating them with rhythmic variations. First, here are the rhythms to be used:

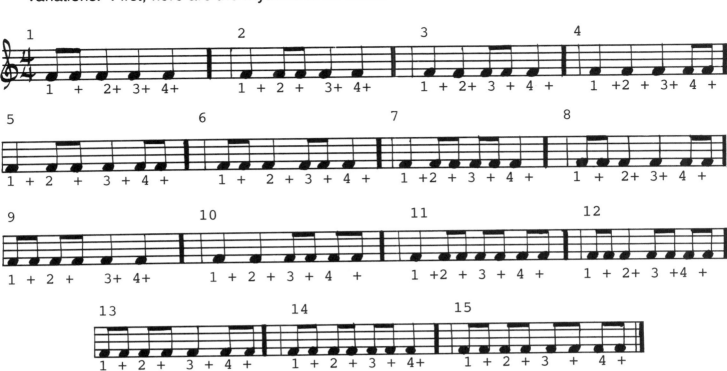

The way these rhythms are to be used is like this: take each rhythmic pattern, and on the beat or beats where eighth notes occur, simply repeat the quarter note on the corresponding beat of each measure in the solo, turning the quarter note or notes into even eighths. Use the same rhythm throughout the solo.

Here are two examples, using rhythm patterns #1 and #5:

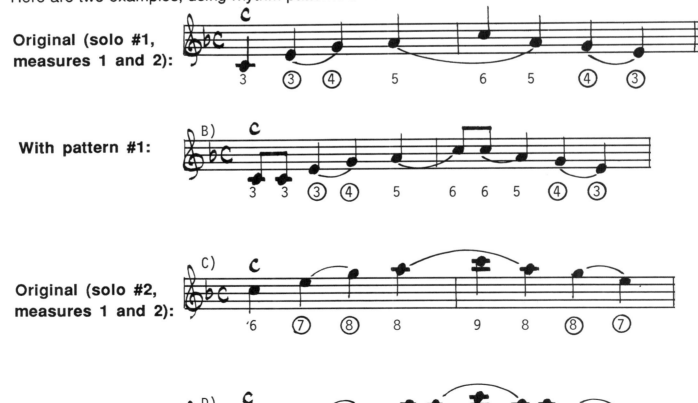

Original (solo #1, measures 1 and 2):

With pattern #1:

Original (solo #2, measures 1 and 2):

With pattern #5:

After you have completed the exercise using even eighths, repeat it using swing eighths instead. If you have any difficulty getting the feel of swing eighths, try playing the eighth notes as triplets first. This idea can be illustrated like this:

Original (solo #1, measure 1)

With pattern #1 in swing eights (as written)

With triplet on first beat

With swing eights (as played)

BASIC RIFFS

The second exercise is a series of thirty one-measure riffs. The first ten of these use quarter and eighth note combinations which by now should be familiar, but without repeating the same tone in a pair of eighth notes. The next twenty riffs feature rhythms that may be new to you - tied eighth and quarter notes, combinations involving rests, triplets, and tied triplets. Riff #30 shows the hemiola, or quarter-note triplet, written out two ways. The first way, using triplets with ties, shows how the hemiola is derived. The second way, #30a, shows how it is written.

The first twenty riffs of this exercise should be done with even as well as swing eigths. The last ten should be done with swing eigths only, as combinations of even eigths and triplets are difficult to get the feel of.

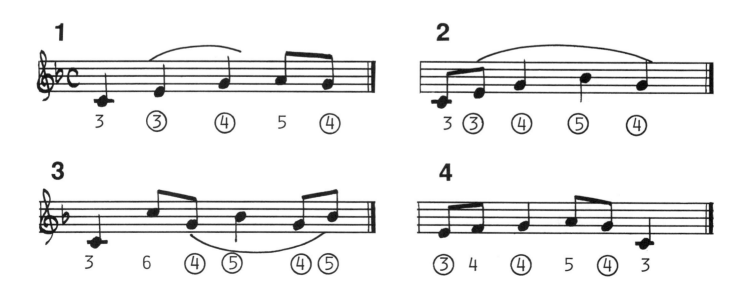

5

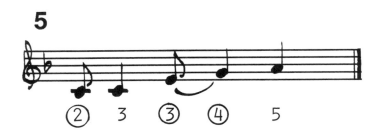

6

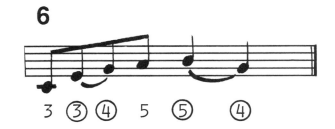

7

8

9

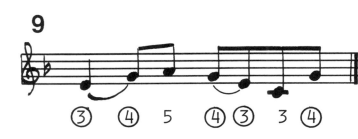

10

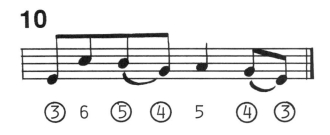

11

12

13

14

15

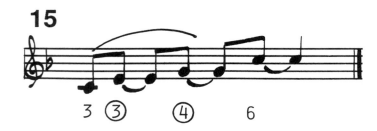

16

17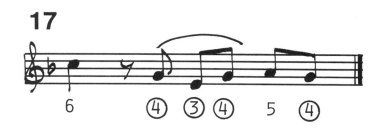

18

19

20

21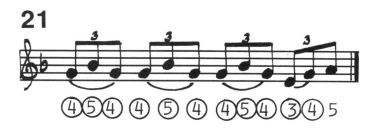

22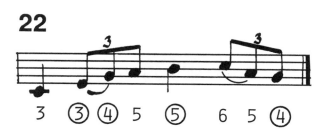

23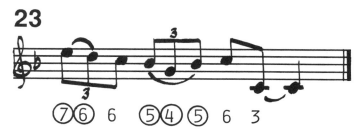

24

25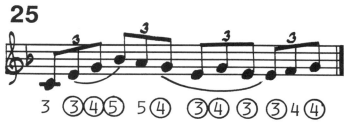

26

27

28

29

30

30a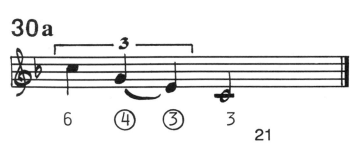

MADCAT

Tony Guerrero

CHAPTER 4

-THE 12 BAR BLUES FORM-

Now that we have discussed music notation and played the first riffs and solos, we can talk about the 12-bar blues form (a bar is another term for a measure) which is the structure or framework of the blues. Literally hundreds of rock, country, folk, jazz and, of course, blues songs--from Hank Williams to the Rolling Stones to Count Basie--have been nothing but 12-bar blues.

12-bar blues is a standardized chord progression (remember, a chord is a group of three or more notes) against which melodies are improvised. Think of the two hands of a piano player, whose left hand plays chords or other forms of accompaniment while the right hand plays melodies. This is exactly how melody and chords work together to create music.

Table 2 illustrates the I, IV and V chords for each key. For example, the note "A" is the first tone of an A major scale, so the A chord is therefore called the I chord. "D" is the fourth step of the A scale, so D is the IV chord. "E" is the fifth step of the A scale, so E is the V chord.

TABLE 2

-KEYS-

I	IV	V
A	D	E
*C	F	G
D	G	A
E	A	B
F	Bb	C
G	C	D

TABLE 3

12 -BAR BLUES

count 1-2-3-4

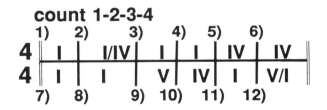

KEY OF C

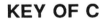

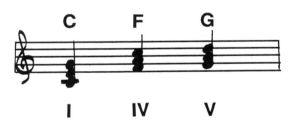

Table 3 shows the chord progression for 12-bar blues in terms of the I, IV and V chords. By substituting the chords in each key for the Roman numerals you can figure out what the 12-bar blues chords in each of the six keys shown in Table 2. For example, in the key of C (marked with an asterisk), the chords would run like this:

$$\| \overset{*}{C} \mid C/F \mid C \mid C \mid F \mid F \mid C \mid C \mid G \mid F \mid C \mid G/C \|$$

You will notice that there are two chords in measures two and twelve. These represent a possible choice of chords. Very often, a IV chord is substituted in the second measure for the I chord (F for C in our example). This is called the "quick change". In the last measure, the V chord is used except for the final chorus, when the I chord is continued as a closing. (Incidentally, there are all kinds of riffs known as "turnarounds" that are used just for the last two measures of the 12-bar form. Examples of these will appear in the solos).

Another way to look at the 12-bar blues form is to know where the chord changes occur in relationship to the vocal line. Blues lyrics are written in a three-line form of verse with the first line repeated once. Here is an example:

| I (1) | IV (2) | I (3) | I (4) |

I'm a Zen Master, baby, I'm gonna fill your void

| IV (5) | IV (6) | I (7) | I (8) |

I'm a Zen Master, baby, I'm gonna fill your void

| V (9) | IV (10) | I (11) | V (12) ||

Well the monks won't know and the Buddha won't get annoyed.

-from "Zen Master Blues," by G. Weiser

In the first line, the opening I chord starts on the first accented word. The following IV and I chords are in parenthesis to show where the changes would be if the quick change variation were used. On the first strong beat of the second line, the IV chord occurs and on the last word of the second line, the harmony returns to the I chord. On the first strong beat of the third line, the V chord occurs. In the middle of the line the IV chord occurs, and on the last word on the third line the harmony resolves to the I chord with the option of returning to V if the verse repeats. The diagonal lines appearing either above the Roman numerals or elsewhere in the verses indicate the positions of the bar lines, and the measures themselves are enumerated by numbers appearing in parentheses.

On the harmonica, the chords to the 12-bar blues can be played like this:

$$\text{I chord} - \begin{bmatrix} 4 \\ 3 \\ 2 \end{bmatrix} \quad \text{IV chord} - \begin{matrix} 6 \\ 5 \\ 4 \end{matrix} \quad \text{and V chord} - \begin{bmatrix} 6 \\ 5 \\ 4 \end{bmatrix}$$

There are other ways to play these chords but these will do for now. Try playing the chords in a quarter note rhythm - one chord per tap of the foot. Use the quick change variation in order to replenish your wind (if you try to play sixteen draw chords in a row you will run out of breath).

You may notice that the V chord does not sound like the I or the IV. This is because on the harmonica the V chord will sometimes have a minor sound, unlike the major sound of the I and IV chords. This will be explained in the following chapter.

Understanding the 12-bar form is essential to good blues improvising because any riff has to relate to the underlying chord. As the chords change, the riffs have to change with them (although it is possible to have some riffs work for two different chords). Even if you are playing solo, unless you know how to change the riffs to suit each on the three different chords of the blues, your playing will not sound like 12-bar blues, however tasteful and polished it may be. This book will teach you everything you will need in order to do this and more.

Solo 3

This solo features eighth note rhythms and has a ragtime flavor to it, particularly in bars 5-8 The rhythm ♪♪♪ could also be written as ♫♫ . Remember that all eighth notes are played as swing eighths unless otherwise indicated. If you have difficulty interpreting any given rhythm, count the time out loud and with your hand tap out the rhythm of the measure in question against your knee. After rehearsing the rhythm in this way, play the measure on the harmonica.

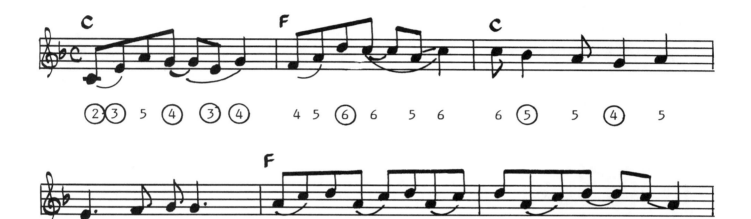

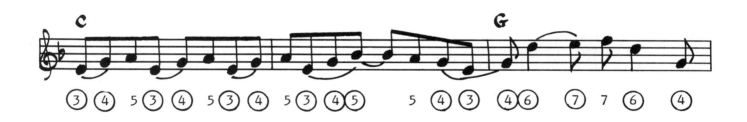

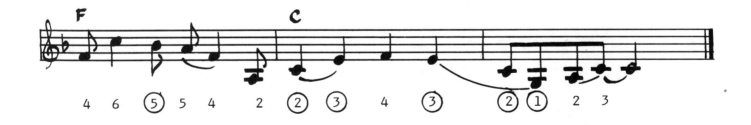

Lee Oskar

CHAPTER 5

-WHAT IS BLUES HARP, EXACTLY?-

When the harmonica is used for blues, it is usually not played in the key you find stamped on it. Instead, it is most often played in the key five steps up (or four steps down) the scale from the keynote. For example, a C scale harmonica would play blues in G. The F scale harmonica used in the written examples plays blues in C. That is why the key signature of F (one flat) is used in our examples, even though the chords C, F & G would suggest the key of C. Because the chord based on the fifth step on the major scale is called the dominant, when we play blues harp we are therefore playing in the dominant key.

TABLE 4

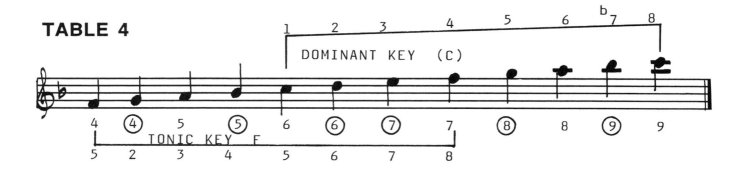

Table 4 shows the difference between the tonic key and the dominant key. The fifth step of the original scale is considered to be the first step of a new scale (which, incidentally, is called the Mixolydian mode). Play the tonic scale on your harmonica, starting from 4-blow and ending at 7-blow. That is the sound of do re mi fa sol la ti do, right? Now play the dominant scale, starting from 6-blow and ending at 9-blow. It does not sound the same as the tonic scale because the seventh tone of the dominant scale is lower than it's position in the tonic scale. This lowered seventh will be referred to as b7, and is one of the "blue" notes of African singing.

Table 5 can be used to determine the dominant or blues key for the seven most commonly used tonic keys (the letter stamped on the harp).

TABLE 5

KEY HARP-BLUES KEY	
A	E
Bb	F
C	G
D	A
E	B
F	C
G	D

TABLE 6

Tonic Key			Dom. Key (blues)		
I	IV	V	I	IV	V
F	Bb	C	C	F	G Minor

Table 6 shows what I, IV and V chords of both the tonic and dominant keys of the F scale harp would look like if they were written out. Notice that the V chord in the key of F is the same as the I chord in the key of C, and that the I chord in F is the same as the IV chord in C.

Our next step is to show you how to figure out what the three notes of each chord would be in both the tonic and dominant keys. For this let us assume that we can start counting from any step in either the tonic or dominant scales. This means that any note can be the first step of a new subscale. (This does not change the key, which is determined by the I chord).

Table 7 shows three possible starting and stopping points within the tonic key: the first, fourth and fifth steps of the scale. If we take the first, third and fifth steps of any of these three scales found within the tonic key, we will have the notes of a **triad,** the most basic kind of complete chord (a two-note chord is incomplete).

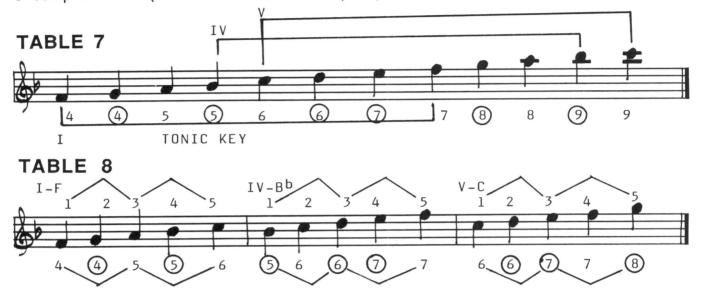

Table 8 shows how the I, IV and V chords of the tonic key are formed. At this point, we can see how the I, IV and V chords each has its own corresponding scale. Whenever the chord changes, the scale changes with it.

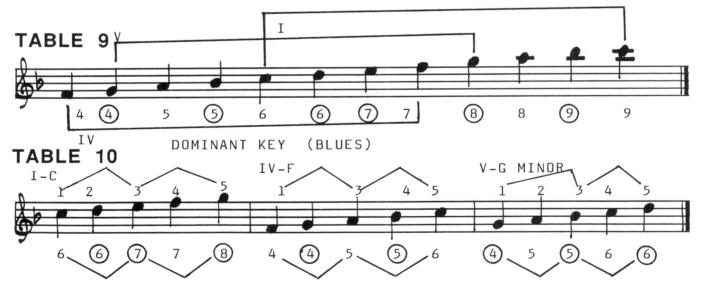

Tables 9 and 10 repeat this process in the dominant key. Here the IV and V chord scales have been transposed down an octave in order to obtain complete scales. Notice that in the dominant key, the V chord is labeled as minor. Even though blues players use major or dominant seventh chords in the accompaniment, the harmonica's minor V chord is an acceptable substitute for either the major or dominant seventh chord. The terms minor, major, etc., will be further explained in Chapter 8.

At this point, it should hopefully be clear how we have arrived at the concept of blues harp as playing in the dominant key, versus playing in the tonic key (which is called "straight harp"). Even though it is possible to play the blues in the tonic key, the dominant key is preferred for this because of the way the low draw notes can be "bent", or lowered, and also the availability of the blue note b7 in the I chord scale, (note bending will be further explained in Chapter 7).

TABLE 11

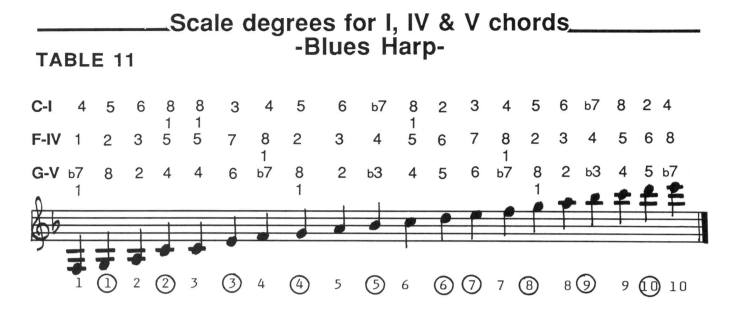

Table 11 shows the same listing of notes on the harmonica as Table 1. This time, however, there are three rows of numbers above the notes listing each note's position in either the I, IV or V chord scales of the dominant key. This means that each note can now have three possible "identities", or relative scale positions, depending on which chord you are playing over. For example, the 2-draw reed would be note 1 (the first step of the scale) if you were playing over the I chord. If you were in the fifth measure of the 12-bar sequence, which is the IV chord, the 2-draw reed would be 5, the fifth scale degree. If you were playing over the V chord, the 2-draw reed would be 4, the fourth step of the V chord scale.

In the first chapter, it was mentioned that the harmonica has a three-octave range with one complete octave in the middle and incomplete lower and upper octaves. By studying Table 11, you can see which notes are missing in the lower and upper octaves. Knowing which notes are missing is just as important as knowing which notes are available. (Later, we will be able to play some of these missing tones by bending the notes). This is all going to determine your choices when you are improvising a riff.

When you look at Table 11, notice also that in each of the three scales 8 and 1 are written one over the other. Even though there are really only seven tones in the basic scale, the first tone of the scale is also considered to be the eighth step of the scale below it. The eighth step of a scale is called the octave. (The term octave also applies to a span or distance of eight notes, which is why the haarmonica is said to have a three octave range). This is why 8 is written over 1. Furthermore, any two notes that are an octave apart will always have the same letter name.

Earlier in this chapter, we talked about one of the "blue" notes-b7. If you look at the V chord scale in Table 11 over the 5-draw reed and the 9-draw reed, you will see that these notes (which are an octave apart), are identified as b3. b3 is another one of the "blue" notes of the African vocal tradition and is a half-step lower than 3.

What is a half step? you may ask. Understanding the concept of a half-step and also that of a whole-step is important to gaining a better knowledge of how scales work. Taking the example of a piano keyboard (as shown in Table 12), notice that the white keys are next to each other at B-C and E-F without a black key in between. B and C and also E and F are therefore a half-step apart. The other white keys-G and A, for example, are a whole step apart.

TABLE 12

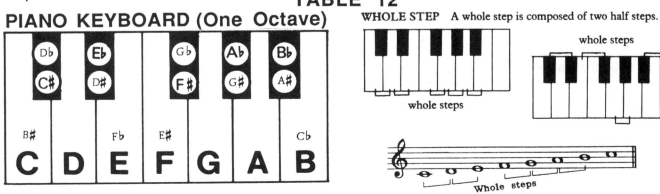

PIANO KEYBOARD (One Octave)

WHOLE STEP   A whole step is composed of two half steps.

If you happen to play the guitar, you may know that a whole step equals the distance of two frets going up or down the neck along the same string, while a half-step equals the distance of one fret.

If you refer back to Table 4, you will see the two scales--the tonic scale beginning on 4-blow (F) and the dominant scale beginning on 6-blow (C). Before, when you played the tonic scale (also called the major scale), you got the sound of "do re mi fa sol la ti do". This is because of the order of whole steps and half-steps, which is; whole step, whole step, half step, whole step, whole step, whole step, half step. In the major or tonic scale then, the half steps are always in between the third and fourth steps and the seventh and eighth steps.

If you play the dominant scale (identified earlier in the chapter as the mixolydian mode), you no longer have the sound of the major scale. This is because the location of one of the half-steps has changed from in between the seventh and eighth tones to in between the sixth and seventh tones. This lowers the seventh tone from its normal position (which we will call ♮7) to b7. b7, as we said before, is one of the "blue" notes.

TABLE 13

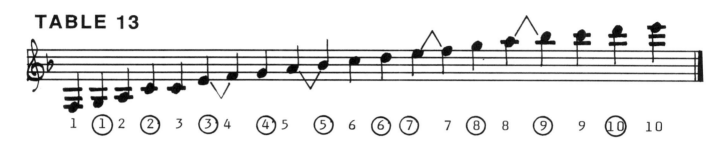

To understand how we arrived at b3, which occurs in the V chord scale shown in Table 11, look at Table 13. This shows the location of all the half steps on the harmonica. Then, on the harmonica play the V chord scale (dominant key), starting on 4-draw and ending on 8-draw. This scale, called the **Dorian mode**, has its half steps located in between the second and the third steps and also in between the sixth and seventh steps.

The position of the first half step in the scale lowers the third step from 3 to b3, giving the Dorian mode (V chord scale) a minor sound. Now we can make the following associations for the dominant key:

I chord - Mixolydian mode (b7) 6-out➔9-out
IV chord - Major scale (no b notes) 4-out➔7-out
V chord - Dorian made (b3, b7) ④ ➔ ⑧

Each of the three chords of the dominant key will have a corresponding scale to be used for soloing. As we go through the 12-bar blues progression, we will know when to use each different scale.

How to use each of the three scales is yet another question. Before we talk about this, let's take a break and play another solo. What is new about Solo No. 4 is that each note is identified in terms of its position in its appropriate scale. The numbers appearing over the staff are the scale degrees. For example, in the first measure, the riff starts on the octave and skips down one octave to note 1, the first degree of the I chord scale. The chord changes to F (IV) in the second measure (this is the "quick change" variation of the 12-bar form) and the first note in the measure is the third step of the IV chord scale which then goes up to the fifth step, back to third, down to the root (the first step is called the root) and so on. This process of labeling each note in a riff or solo, according to its position in its respective scale (I, IV, or V), is called a **melodic analysis**, and will become very useful when we start laying down guidelines for improvisation, and illustrating these guidelines with sample riffs and solos.

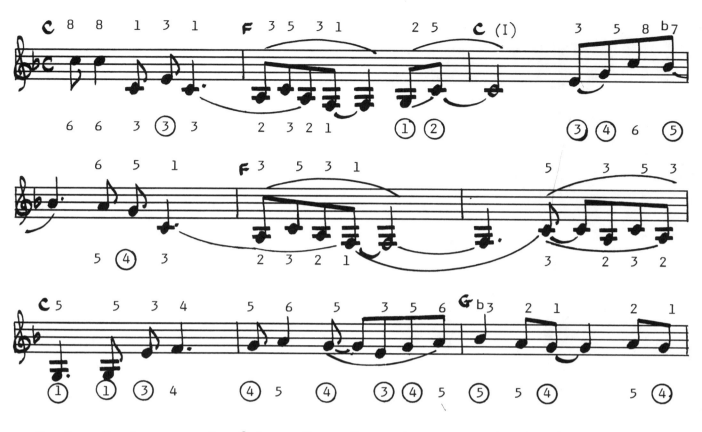

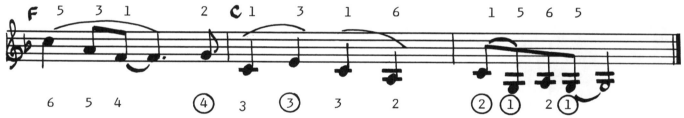

Darrell Mansfield

CHAPTER 6

LEARNING YOUR WAY AROUND THE HARMONICA

Before we start talking about note bending, improvisation and special harmonica techniques, we need to become more familiar with the locations of the notes on the harmonica in terms of scale degrees. In Chapter Three it was stated that knowing the letter names of the notes is not particularly important because they will change according to the key of the harp you are playing. But what is essential to good blues improvising is to always know two things: first, the chord you are playing over and second, what step of either of the three scales you are on. Keeping track of which chord you are on is obviously going to be easier, because the chords usually will not change as often as the notes.

SCALE DEGREES FOR 1, IV & V CHORDS (Dominant Key)

TABLE 14

Draw or In Reeds ◯

	1	2	3	4	5	6	7	8	9	10
I	5	1(8)	3	5	b7	2	3	5	b7	2
IV	2	5	7	2	4	6	7	2	4	6
V	1(8)	4	6	1(8)	b3	5	6	1(8)	b3	5

TABLE 14a

Blow or Out Reeds

	1	2	3	4	5	6	7	8	9	10
I	4	6	1(8)	4	6	1(8)	4	6	1(8)	4
IV	1	3	5	1(8)	3	5	1(8)	3	5	1
V	b7	2	4	b7	2	4	b7	2	4	b7

Table 14 presents the same information as Table 14a, but from a different point of view. Here the written notes have been dispensed with, and the scale degrees are listed according to the needs only. Using this table we can begin learning to think in terms of scale degrees.

There is a useful series of excercises for this which I call "melodic sequences". Here's how they work: You will be given sequences of four scale degrees each which represent four quarter notes in four-four time. You will then be told chord or chords with which they can be played. Next you will find the notes on the harmonica corresponding to the scale degrees in the sequence. Very often, it will be possible to play any given sequence in more than one octave. When this is the case, learn the sequence in as many octaves as possible.

Here are some examples:
1) I- 1 3 5 6   solution: ② ③ ④ 5 or 6 ⑦ ⑧ 8
First, the fact that this is a I chord riff means that you read only the top rows of each of the two parts of Table 14. Scale degree 1 in the I chord row is ②. (It is also 3-out, but we will use ② this time). Scale degree 3 is found in the top or I chord row under ③. Scale degree 5 is found in the top row under ④. Scale degree 6 is found in the "blow" part of the diagram, top row, under hole 5. Repeating the process to find the same riff in the upper octave, we still read only the top row, and see that 1 is now found in the 6-out column. 3 is found in the ⑦ column, 5 is found under ⑧, and 6 is found under 8-out. Now play the riff.

2) **IV- 1 3 4 5 solution: 4 5 ⑤ 6 or 7 8 ⑨ 9**

For the IV chord, all we have to do is repeat the procedure we used for the first example using the middle rows of each part of the diagram instead of the top rows.

3) **V- 8 b7 6 5 solution: ⑧ 7 ⑦ ⑥**

Now, we have scale degree 8, which is the same as 1. Remember that scale degree 1 is the eighth step of the lower octave. This is going to be a descending riff, unlike the first two which were ascending.

Repeat the same process you used for the first example using the bottom rows only. This riff can only be played in one octave.

After you have learned all the riffs, try experimenting with some different rhythms to liven them up. Using swing eighths, ties and triplets, for example can turn any one of the following exercises into an exciting riff.

---

1) Exercises for the I, IV and V chords.

These sequences can be played with each of the three chords. First, find the riffs in the top rows (I chord). Then, in the middle rows (IV chord), and then in the bottom rows (V chord).

A plus sign (+) over a scale degree indicates it is in the higher octave.

For example: I- 5 8 $\overset{+}{3}$ 8   **solution:** ④ 6 ⑦ 6

| 1215 | 1251 | 1256 | 1521 | 1258 | 1565 | 1656 | 1568 | 1658 |
| 1545 | 1856 | | | | | | | |

| 1865 | 1585 | 5456 | 5651 | 5451 | 5865 | 5685 | 5856 | 5215 |
| 5145 | 5658 | | | | | | | |

| 5156 | 5158 | 8656 | 8565 | 8651 | 8545 | 8515 | 8156 | 8165 |

$\overset{+}{}$

| 8145 | 8121 | 8521 | 5828 |

---

2) Exercise for the I and IV chords

| 1231 | 1321 | 1323 | 1232 | 1234 | 1434 | 1345 | 1543 | 1353 | 1535 |
| 1356 | 1358 | 1653 | | | | | | | |

| 1538 | 1853 | 1835 | 3213 | 3123 | 3431 | 3543 | 3653 | 3134 | 3456 |
| 3135 | 3565 | 3656 | | | | | | | |

| 3586 | 3651 | 3531 | 3858 | 3531 | 3538 | 3851 | 3545 | 5653 | 5134 |
| 5313 | 5431 | 5323 | | | | | | | |

| 5653 | 5156 | 5356 | 5345 | 5435 | 6583 | 6545 | 6536 | 6535 | 6853 |
| 8135 | 8543 | 8356 | | | | | | | |

| 8365 | 8351 | 8153 | $\overset{+}{5838}$ | $\overset{+}{5386}$ | $\overset{+}{8385}$ | $\overset{+}{3858}$ | $\overset{+}{3281}$ | $\overset{+}{3565}$ | $\overset{+}{3656}$ |

$\overset{+}{3545}$

3)   Exercises for the I and V chords.

156b7   1b765   165b7   1b75b7   1b78b7   18b75   158b7   1b756
185b7   5b78b7

58b78   515b7   58b75   b78b75   56b76   5b76b7   58b76   586b7
b765b7   b756b7

b7515   8b756   856b7   86b78   8b751   815b7   8b765   8b75b7

---

4)   Exercises for the IV chord.   +   +
5878   8785   5678   8765   5781   3578   8785   7828   7838   7865
7813

---

5)   Exercises for the V chord.
12b31   16341   14b31   1b34b3   1b35b3   15b34   15b35   1b345
154b3   1b35b7

15b34   12b35   b345b3   b31b35   b354b3   b356b3   b35b75
b38b75   b385b7

5b31b3   54b31   54b38   b754b3   b785b3   8b75b3   85b31
8b785   8b78b3
         +   +   +   +   +
8b78b3   58b35   8b38b7   85b35   b78b38

It will probably take you a little time to get through all five series of exercises, but "you've gotta pay your dues to play the blues." If you apply yourself to these exercises, you will know your way around the harp better than some people who have been playing it for years.

Anyway, after all this technical stuff, it is time to have some fun. Here is another solo for you. Solo 5 has the scale degrees marked over the staff as did Solo 4. Notice the note G (④) that ties over from the sixth to the seventh measure. That note was scale degree 2 of the IV chord, but when the chord changed, it became scale degree 5 of the I chord.

Solo 5

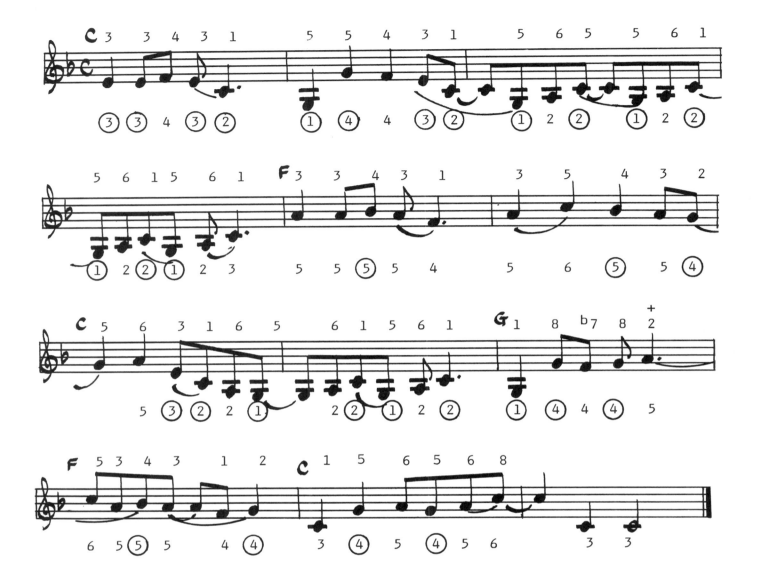

36

Junior Wells

CHAPTER 7

-NOTE BENDING-

Note bending- the technique of lowering the pitch of the notes by changing the shape of your mouth- is the next thing you need to learn. Note bending is probably the most soulful thing about blues harp playing and is undoubtedly responsible for much of its appeal. Once mastered, this technique will enable you to play several notes that were previously unavailable on the harmonica.

Note bends can be done on the lower six draw reeds and on the upper four blow reeds. Bending the draw reeds is called **overdrawing** and bending the blow reeds is called **overblowing.** Overdrawing is easier to begin with so we will start with that. This technique can be elusive at first so just keep trying if your initial attempts are not successful.

When you bend a note, your mouth changes in the following way: **1)** your jaw lifts; **2)** your tongue lowers in front and rises in back; **3)** the back of your throat opens up; **4)** the breath is drawn from the belly; and **5)** your lips tense slightly.

When all this is done correctly, the note will lower. What actually happens inside the harmonica is that the air stream has narrowed, and instead of the tip of the reed vibrating as usual, the thicker part (which vibrates more slowly and therefore at a lower pitch) is activated. If you allow your mouth to resume its normal playing position as you are playing a bent note, the pitch will rise and return to normal. This process of bending and releasing a note bend can be done quickly or slowly.

If you do have trouble bending the note, there are two things you can do to get the feel of how the mouth and the tongue in particular changes position: **1)** Say "boy.", Then say "oy," then "oy-oy-oy." **2)** Whistle a note that is somewhere in the middle of your range. Then, continue to whistle and let the pitch drop down as far as possible. Then, while inhaling, repeat the process.

④ and ⑤ are probably the easiest notes to get started on. Try these at first and then try ① , ② , ③ , & ⑥ .

How much the hole can be lowered depends on which reed you are playing. ① , ④ , ⑤ and ⑥ can only be lowered by a half-step. ② can be lowered by a half-step or a whole-step and ③ can be lowered by a half-step, a whole-step or even a minor third (a whole and a half-step). ③ can also be the toughest one to bend in the beginning so save it for last. Remember, breathe through your nose if you cannot get a good tone on ③ .
When a note is to be bent by a half-step, it will look like this: ②↓

Whole-step bends will look like this: ②↡ .

The minor third bend on ③ (which rarely occurs) looks like this: ③↡↓

Table 15 - Note Bends

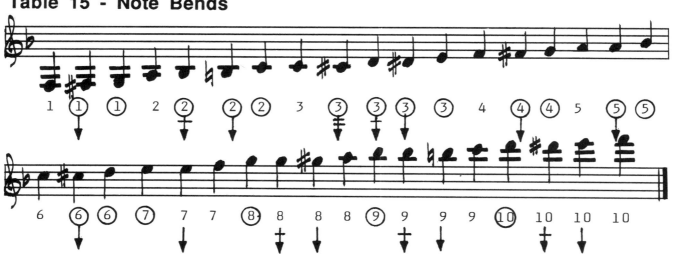

Table 15 shows the note bends on the F scale harp. Table 16 illustrates the idea of "enharmonic equivalents." For example, F# is the same as Gb. This is important to know because the same note could be written either way in the riffs and solos which follow.

Enharmonic Equivalents

TABLE 16

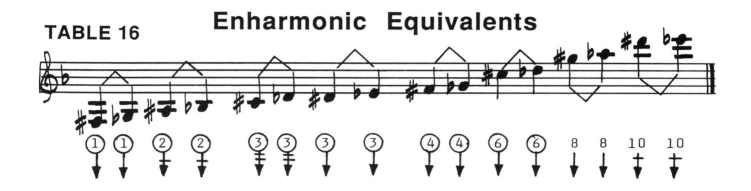

TABLE 17-Complete Scale Degree Chart for I, IV & V Chords.

Draw Reeds ◯

	1	2	3	4	5	6	7	8	9	10
I	5	1	3	5	b7	2	3	5	b7	2
1/2 bend	b5	7	b3	b5	6	b2				
whole bend		b7	2							
1 1/2 bend			b2							
I V	2	5	7	2	4	6	7	2	4	6
1/2 bend	b2	b5	b7	b2	3	b6				
whole bend		4	6							
1 1/2 bend			b6							
V	1	4	6	1	b3	5	6	1	b3	5
1/2 bend	7	3	b6	7	2	b5				
whole bend		b3	5							
1 1/2 bend			b5							

Blow Reeds

	1	2	3	4	5	6	7	8	9	10
I	4	6	1	4	6	1	4	6	1	4
1/2 bend							3	b6	7	3
whole bend							5	b7	b3
I V	1	3	5	1	3	5	1	3	5	1
1/2 bend							7	b3	b5	7
whole bend							2	4	b7
V	b7	2	4	b7	2	4	b7	2	4	b7
1/2 bend							6	b2	3	6
whole bend							1	b3	b6

Table 17 illustrates all the notes available on the harmonica, including note bends, in terms of scale degrees for the I, IV and V chords. In any reed where more than one number appears, the top number represents the unbent note. The numbers below it represent the pitch when bent down to a half-step, whole-step or minor third (③ only).

Table 17 introduces three new notes--b2, b5 and b6. b2 is in between 1 and 2 in the scale, b5, which is a "blue"note, is in between 4 and 5, and b6 is in between 5 and 6. If you got through the melodic sequence exercises in the last chapter, integrating these new scale degrees into your thinking should not be that hard. <u>Here are some new sequences for note bends</u>

I chord -   5b543   87b76   8b765   8b758   3b321   3213   3b32b2   2b285^{+ +}

b765b7-higher octave only   8#7b75

IV chord - 87b76   32b21   86b65   1431   5451   5b543   5431

V chord - 87b78   43b34   8b78b7   6543   5b54b3

As you can see, sometimes you will only have to bend a note by a half-step and sometimes by a whole-step. Whole-step bends are more difficult in the beginning. If you play another instrument, try playing the sequences on the other instrument first and then try them on the harmonica. This way, you will know what they are supposed to sound like.

Also, quarter-step bends are possible on the harmonica and are commonly used. This practice has its roots in the West African vocal scale, where the "blue" 3rd was really a note that hovered in between b3 and #3 (the "blue" 7th was more of a correct b7 and the "blue" fourth was close to b5). The note-bending capabilities of the harmonica make it possible to play a true "blue" 3rd, a note you'll need to recognize and know how to play.. You might try taking some I chord melodic sequence exercises containing either #3 or b3 and try using "blue" 3 instead, bending ③ down a quarter step. "Blue" 5ths are also sometimes heard as quarter step bends on ① and ④.

Solo 6 includes note bends. In all cases, you will be starting from the unbent note and lowering the pitch, sometimes allowing it to return to normal. When a note bend appears for the first time, the scale degree of the note will be given in terms of the I, IV or V chord.

Solo 6

The next thing we need to learn about note bends is how to play a reed with the note already bent. To begin a note with the pitch already lowered, your mouth has to change into the bending position just before you start the note. The throat has to open up this time as if saying the name "KAY" while inhaling. Try bending ④ down to ④ a few times.

Listen to the pitch of ④ and remember what your mouth was doing to bend the note.

Then jump from ③ to ④

Solo No. 7 has been written to develop the technique of hitting a bent note directly without first lowering it from the normal pitch. This solo is to be played at a slow tempo and has triplets. By now you should know when to tongue or connect adjacent in or out reeds with the same breath, so the breath lines have been omitted.

Solo 7

Bending the high out reeds (overblowing) is done by raising the middle of the tongue as you blow. To help get the hang of this, you can invert the whistling exercise by whistling a note that is somewhere in the middle of your range and letting it rise as high as it can go.

Table 17 shows that it is possible to bend 7-out down a half step and 8, 9 and 10-out down a half step or a whole step. At first, hitting an overblown bent note directly is difficult to the point of being impractical, so any riffs you will want to play using overblowing should start on the normal tone first. There are a lot of IV chord riffs that work well with overblowing as it is easy to start on 3, 5 or 8, bend down to the "blue" note (b3, b5 or b7) and either allow the pitch to return to normal or go from the bent note to another reed.

Here are some sequences for hitting a bent note directly. Play these in the lower reeds only.

I chord - 34b55   12b33   5b778   2b315   5b765

IV chord - 1b551   1b765   1451   1431   14b55   5b778   156b7   2b28b7 (+)

V chord - b7783 (+)   56b75   b5585   8565   8b756   835b7

Here are some sequences for overblown note bends:

I chord - 4365   4321   6543   87b75   8b765

IV chord - 8783 (+)   3b331   5b556   5453   87b75   8b785

V chord - b765b7   b328b7 (++)   5431   b765b7   2b28b7 (+ +)

Charlie Musslewhite

James Cotton

CHAPTER 8

-HOW TO IMPROVISE-

Blues and rock are largely improvisational forms of music, which means that the riffs and solos are created on the spot by the performer. In the early days of the blues (and even yet in some places, I'm sure) the lyrics, melodies and even the chord changes of the songs were improvised, as was the instrumental accompaniment. Later on, the chord changes became standardized when blues players formed bands rather than performing as soloists.

Improvisation is a skill that takes time to learn. At first, most solos are usually more or less pre-planned but over the course of time they tend to become increasingly spontaneous. Personality also shows through, and many blues artists have evolved such a highly individualized playing style that they can be recognized after only a few measures of a solo.

In order to develop an ear for good soloing, you should listen as much as possible to harp players in addition to the time spent playing. Try to find records of bands featuring harmonica. The early albums of the Beatles, Rolling Stones and the Grateful Dead, for example, all feature harmonica solos. You will also need records of the original masters of blues harp--players such as Sonny Terry, Sonny Boy Williamson, James Cotton, Junior Wells, Big Walter, Little Walter, Charlie Musslewhite and Paul Butterfield (see Discography).

In this chapter, you will be given rules for improvisation which apply with equal validity to the I, IV and V chords. These rules are not to be considered ironclad, but rather flexible guidelines to which exceptions will sometimes be found. (Usually, the exceptions will have some kind of justifying logic--for example, playing a I chord riff over the IV or V chord).

The rules of improvisation will be presented in three stages and sample riffs and solos given to illustrate the various points made. Before you start studying the rules, you should do three things: **1)** Review the exercises at the end of Chapter 6; **2)** Study Table 17 and know which note bends correspond with which scale degrees in each of the I, IV and V scales; and **3)** Study solos 4 and 5, and analyze all the other solos in the same way using a pencil to write in the scale degree above each note. Use Table 17 as a reference. This last exercise in particular is very useful, as the rules will make more sense if you can study an abundance of examples. Also, when you start to work out riffs concentrate on the six lower reeds, which is where most riffs and solos are played, Later on you can explore the high register.

Part 1
-PENTATONIC SCALES-

The simplest kind of scales that can be used for soloing are pentatonic scales. Pentatonic means five-toned and we will be using two different pentatonic scales: the **pentatonic minor** (1b345b78) which omits the second and sixth tones, and the **pentatonic major** (123 568) which omits the fourth and seventh tones. The omission of these tones creates leaps within the scales (a leap is any distance greater than a whole-step). Pentatonic scales also called "gapped" scales. We will start with minor form.

Here are the guidelines for their use.
PENTATONIC MINOR
● **1.** 1, b3, 5 and 8 are chord tones and 4 and b7 are non-chord tones.

This distinction is all-important. Along with phrasing, good improvising depends on understanding the relationship between chord tones and non-chord tones. 1, b3 and 5 (8 is the high1) make up the notes of the minor chord. Even though the 12-bar blues form uses major chords (1, 3 and 5 are the notes of the major chord), it is still all right to use b3 in the melody over 3 in the accompaniment. b3 here functions as a substitute for 3.

● **2.** A chord-tone may progress to any note in the scale or may repeat, but a non-chord tone, if it does not repeat, must go to a chord-tone, which will usually be a neighboring one. This means that 4 will usually go to 5 or b3, and that b7 will usually go to 5 or 8. Non-chord tones are commonly classified in different ways according to how they behave. When a non-chord tone is found in between two chord tones that are three or four steps apart, it is called a passing tone. For example, in the progression b345, or 54b3, 4 would be considered a passing tone.

In addition to passing tones, non-chord tones are also described as auxiliary tones when they occur in two other types of situations. The first type of auxiliary tone is found above or below two of the same chord tones. This is also called a neighboring tone.

For example, in the progressions 5b75 and 8b78, b7 would be neighboring tone. Similarly, in the progressions b34b3 and 545, 4 would be neighboring tone.

The second type of auxiliary tone is approached by a leap and resolves to a neighboring chord tone. The progressions, 14b3, 145, 845, 84b3, 1b75, 1b78, and b3b78 would all be examples of this type of auxillary tone, which is also referred to as an appoggiatura.

As well as passing and auxillary tones there are also the escape tone, which is approached by step and left by leap, and the free tone, which is approached and left by leap. Examples of these would be the progressions 8b7b3, b348, and 541 in the case of the escape tone, and 1b71 or 848 in the case of the free tone.

Other kinds of non-chord tones will be discussed later. When you first start to improvise, allow the non-chord tones to go to neighboring chord tones, only, as either auxillary or passing tones. Then after you can improvise within this limitation and always know which scale degree you are on, try following b7 with b3 or 1 or following 4 with 1 or 8. When a non-chord tone goes to a non-adjacent chord tone the melody should change direction. This rule also tends to apply when a chord tone goes to a non-adjacent chord tone (1 to 8, for example), or when a chord-tone skips to a non-chord tone. For example, 1b75 would sound better than 1b78. Remember that your ear should be the final judge. Play what sounds good.

● **3.** Avoid long notes on 4 (more than a quarter or dotted quarter note). A long note on 4 does not jive with the accompaniment and creates a false suggestion of a chord change. For example. if you are with a band and you are soloing over the I chord, and you play a half note on scale degree 4, it will seem as though the rhythm section has missed a change to the IV chord.

● **4.** Riffs ending on b3, 5 or b7 create the impression of a comma at the end of a phrase, and riffs ending on 1 or 8 create the impression of a period at the end of a sentence. 1 and 8 are notes of resolution--the places where the melody "comes home". Most songs or tunes end on the tonic or octave. Music, like speech, occurs in phrases--some conclusive and some not. Phrases ending on b3, 5 or b7 create tension and phrases ending on 1 or 8 resolve this tension. The creation and resolution of tension is a basic principle of melody.

In the blues, the melody will almost always go to 1 or 8 on the first beat of measure 11 (I chord). In measure 12, first beat, the melody will also usually go to 1 or 8.

It is important to note that the pentatonic minor is only possible for the I and V chords and not for the IV chord. In the lower octave of the IV chord, b3 in unavailable (although b7 is) and in the upper octave, b3 cannot easily be hit directly as it is an overblown bent note. In the upper octave of the I chord, the pentatonic minor is also impossible. Therefore, when you practice, just try out I or V chord riffs without trying to follow the 12-bar blues pattern. You will be able to use the 12-bar pattern as soon as you learn the pentatonic major scale, which will enable you to complete the pattern with chord riffs.

● **5.** A good riff should be singable and should not progress too far in one direction (an octave or less).

This rule holds for any riff developed out of any scale. To explain this further, it should be said that a good melody is usually a balanced combination of steps and leaps. In the first stage of improvising, the leaps should only start from the chord tones (**Rule 2**). The main purpose of the non-chord tones, on the other hand, is to connect the chord tones. If a riff has too much step-wise motion, it may sound tedious; if it has too much leapwise motion, it may sound disjointed. Also, a riff usually should not progress further than an octave without changing direction and more likely will change direction sooner than that. In the first two measures of solo 11, however, the opening riff climbs up a distance of two octaves. Because the second half of the phrase is only a repetition of the first half, an octave higher, the riff works. Here are some riffs in the pentatonic minor for the I and V chords. The melodic analysis has been given.

Pentatonic Minor Riffs

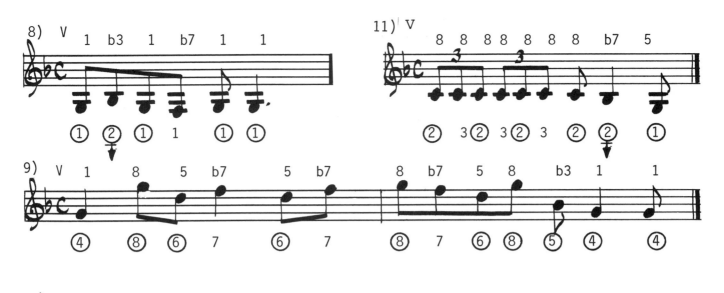

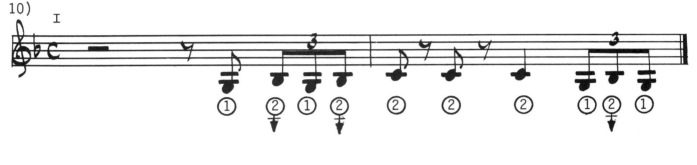

PENTATONIC MAJOR

The pentatonic major (1 2 3 5 6 8) has more of a folk or country sound than the pentatonic minor, which has more of a blues or rock sound. The rules are similar to those for the pentatonic minor.

● **6.** 1, 3, 5 and 8 are chord tones and 2 and 6 are non-chord tones.   1, 3 and 5 are the notes of a major chord.

● **7.** A chord tone may go to any note (skip or step) or repeat, but a non-chord tone if it does not repeat must go to a chord tone, which will usually be a neighboring chord tone.

This is identical to **Rule 2**. 6 will go to 5 or 8 and 2 will go to 1 or 3. Later, 6 can leap to 3 or 1. However, leaps from 2 to 5 or 8 usually do not sound right. (Exception--something like 15 25 35 15, where the 2-5 leap is a part of a longer sequence.) 2 and 6 can be used as auxiliary or passing tones.

● **8.** Long notes on 2 or 6 have a jazzy sound and are allowed, but are better avoided at first.

The sixth chord (1 3 5 6) and dominant ninth chord (1 3 5 b7 2) are commonly substituted for the usual major and dominant seventh (1 3 5 b7) chords that accompany the blues, so long notes on 2 or 6 when used sparingly will often work. Avoid these long notes in the beginning and follow the rule of limiting the progression of the non-chord tones to the neighboring chord-tones only. After that, you can experiment.

● **9.** Phrases ending on 3 and 5 are like the comma at the end of a phrase, and phrases ending on 1 or 8 are like the period at the end of a sentence. This is similar to **Rule 4** and the idea of tension and resolution applies in the same way.

On the harmonica, the pentatonic major is impossible in the upper octave of the V chord. In the lower octave of the V chord, it is playable, but not easy, because going from 3 to 5 in the scale involves going from ② to ③ which requires good note bending technique. The pentatonic major is playable in the I and IV chords. Here are some riffs in the pentatonic major scale with analysis:

Pentatonic Major Riffs

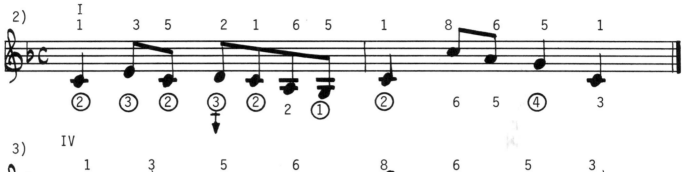

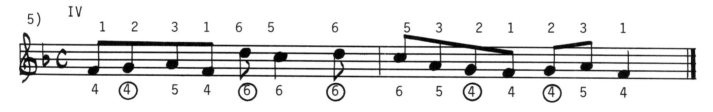

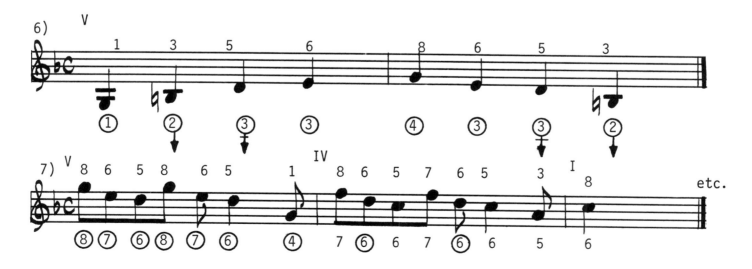

48

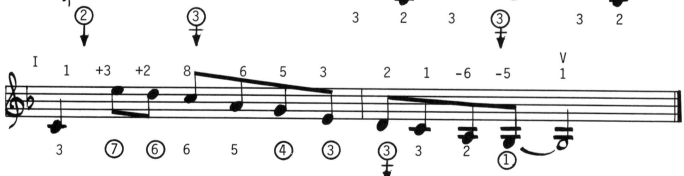

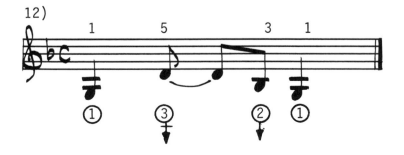

49

In addition to the sequence exercises at the end of Chapter 6 and the melodic analysis of the solos, another helpful exercise for developing improvisational skills is to take the rhythm of any measure or two and use different notes in a sequence that follows the rules. This exercise should be done not only for the pentatonic scales but also for the other two stages of improvisation which follow. Using the rhythm of any one measure (or more), dozens of new riffs will be possible. Try starting riffs on 1, then on b3 or 3, then on 5, and then on 8. After that, try starting some riffs on non-chord tones. Then use the same sequence of scale degrees as the original measure or measures, by this time change the rhythm. Another good exercise for improvising is to stay on one chord and just concentrate on creating and resolving tensions. Play a two-measure phrase ending on b3, 3, 5 or b7 and then follow it with a phrase endng on 1 or 8. Do this with the I, IV and V chords separately. Vary the rhythms and avoid repeating yourself.

Part II
THE COMBINED SCALE (12 b3 3 4 5 6 b7 8)

When we put the two pentatonic scales together, the result is something I call the "combined" scale. All the pentatonic rules will still hold but there will, of course, be new possibilities. 2 can now be used as a passing note in between 1 and b3 (or vice versa) or as an auxiliary note to b3. 4 can be a passing note between 3 and 5, or as an auxiliary note to 3.

1. b3 and 3 are interchangeable if not used consecutively. If b3 and 3 are used consecutively, 3 can follow b3 and progress to any note. If b3 follows 3, it must progress to 2 or return to 3.

For example, the sequence 3 b3 3 1 will sound like blues but the sequence b3 3 b3 1 will create what I call the "Twilight Zone Effect." Avoid it and any other melodic sequence that breaks this rule. (3 b3 5, etc.) The subtle balance of the major and minor qualities is an important aspect of the blues. Breaking Rule #1 will tilt a riff too far towards the minor side of things. However, 3 b3 2 1 is fine, or 3 b3 2 3, or 2 6 b3 3, ect. Notice how 2 will usually go only to 1, b3 or 3 in this type of situation, rather than leap to a chord tone.

● 2. b3 can progress to 6 and 3 can progress to b7. 3 - b7 will sound better than b3 - 6, which will tend to suggest the IV chord because b3 and 6 of the I chord are the same notes as 3 and b7 of the IV chord. 3 and b7 are a stronger combination than b3 and 6. Thus, the IV chord is suggested, but both are possible. Listen to this:

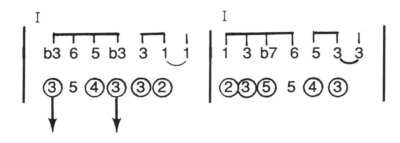

Very often changing direction after leaps like these will make a riff work better, as shown in the examples.

● 3. 6 and b7 are interchangeable and can be used freely together. Long notes on b7 are more common than those on 6 and will usually work better.

The first stage of working with this rule is to allow 6 to go to 5, b7 or 8 and to allow b7 to go to 6, 5 or 8. Later, leaps from 6 or b7 to 1, b3 or 3 can be used. (Here again, a change of direction after a wide leap will often help.) There are many classic blues riffs involving combinations of 5, 6 and b7. Try these:

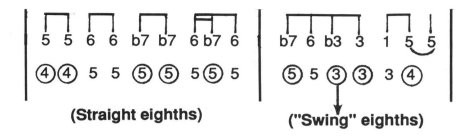

(Straight eighths)   **("Swing" eighths)**

● **4**. A leap from b7 up or down to 2, or from 2 to b7 will work, as it suggests a dominant ninth chord. b7 may also progress to 4 if 4 is followed by 5, b3, or 3.

These situations could be explained either as non-chord tones progressing to other non-chord tones or as non-chord tones temporarily assuming the status of chord-tones (much like the letter "y" in the alphabet, which can either act as a consonant or a vowel) and there-fore being able to move to any note in the scale. Thus in the progressions b2 b7 8, b7 4 b3, 2 6 b7, etc,. The middle tone in each group of three could be viewed as an appoggiatura in between two chord tones.

The ceasura, or pause in the melody, as another case where a non-chord tone could progress to another non-chord tone. If a phrase ends on a non-chord tone and there is then a ceasura, the musical train of thought has been broken and the melody is free to resume anywhere in the scale. The ceasura is common in Chicago blues.

Also, 6 may occasionally progress to 4 and vice-versa, in situations where the melody is moving in successive thirds. Here are some examples:

```
       I      (IV)  (I)   (IV)          I      (IV)      (I)
                                               3       3
1) 3 5  4 6   5 b7  4 6       2) b7 5 b7  6 4 6  3 5 5
   ③④ 4 5    ④⑤ 4 5          ⑤④⑤ 5 4 5 ③④
```

```
       I           (IV)      (I)
            3         3
3)  3 5 3   4 6 4     3 1 1
    ③④③ 4 5 4 ③ 3
```

The riffs presented above will be easier to understand if we introduce the idea of passing chords and auxiliary chords. These are simply an extension of the idea of passing and auxiliary notes.

In example 1, 3 and 5 of the I chord, which are a third apart, go to 4 and 6, which are the same as 1 and 3 of the IV chord. 5 and b7 of the I chord follow, and riff returns to 4 and 6. 4 and 6 used together in this way suggest the IV chord, and thus may be called a passing chord.

In Example 2 what is basically the reverse of Example 1, with the riff descending instead of ascending. 4 and 6 are again acting as a passing chord.

In Example 3, 4 and 6 are acting as an auxiliary rather than a passing chord. It is important to note that a passing or auxiliary chord does not represent a shift in the overall harmony but rather movement within the chord that does not change it. This is why the first I chord designation appearing at the beginning of each example is not in parenthesis as are the rest of the chord designations.

Also, 2 and 4 can be used in the same way as 4 and 6, making possible sequences such as 13 24 35 24, 31 42 31, etc. 2 and 4 here represent a passing or auxiliary V7 chord (2 and 4 of the I chord are the same as 5 and b7 of the V7 chord). These kinds of riffs can also be done within the IV and V chords as well as the I chord.

There were leaps in the pentatonic scales (1 to b3, 5 to b7 in minor, 3 to 5, 6 to 8 in major) but with the combined scale, complete stepwise motion is possible, at least in theory. On the harmonica, however the complete combined scales are only possible in the lower octaves of the I and V chords. Study Table 17 to find the possibilities, and remember to analyze the solos. Here are some riffs for the combined scale with analysis.

Combined Scale Riffs

I chord

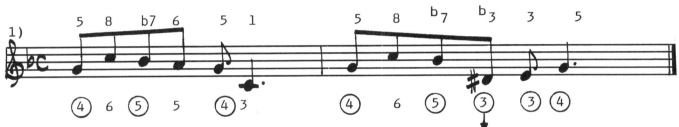

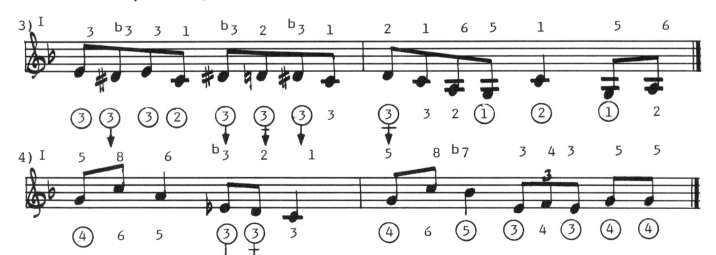

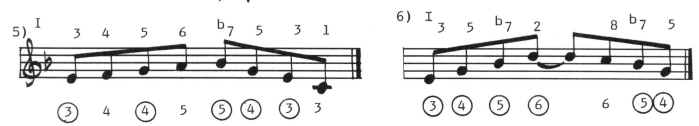

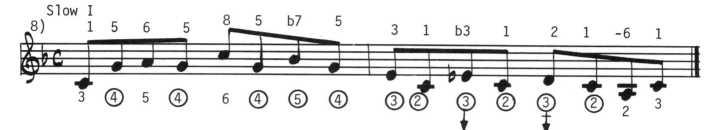

In addition to scales, modes, and chords, another important concept in music the arpeggio or broken chord. If we play 2-in, 3-in, and 4-in, at the same time, we have the I chord. However, it is also possible to play the notes of the I chord. separately, for instance 1-3-5-3, 5-1-3-1, 8-5-3-1, 3-5-8-3, etc. Bugle calls, for example, are all various major chord arpeggios. It is furthermore possible to have arpeggios derived from any type of chord, although for the purpose of blues and rock improvising we shall restrict ourselves almost entirely to the major (1-3-5), minor (1-b3-5) dominant seventh (1-3-5-b7) and minor seventh (1-b3-5-b7) chords.

Here are two guidelines for using arpeggios. Four or more non-repeating chord-tones used consecutively will serve as a working definition of an arpeggio.

  1.   Arpeggios should be used sparingly. The importance of non-chord tones should be remembered.

  2.   At first, do not proceed more than an octave in one direction.

If you have completed the melodic analysis of the solos in this book, study them again, this time looking for arpeggios. In solo #4, for example, arpeggios can be found in the second and third measures.

Part III

Using b2, b5, b6, and 7

When we add these four new notes to the combined scale, we have a complete half-step or chromatic scale (1 b2 2 b3 3 4 b5 5 b6 6 b7 7 8). Even though these notes are found here and there on the harmonica, the diatonic harmonica cannot really play a chromatic scale. This was why the chromatic harmonica was invented in 1918. If you study Table 17, you can find the gaps in each of the I, IV and V chord scales. It should be said that b2 and b6 are the least used tones and are mostly used in riffs that connect two different chords. b5 and 7, on the other hand, have a variety of uses. Here are the guidelines for their use.

● 1. Avoid long notes on b2, b6 or 7. This is similar to Part 1, Rule 3.

● 2. When a chord is about to change, and the melody is leaving a chord tone and going to a chord tone of the second chord that is whole step apart from the chord tone of the first chord, the tone in between may be used. For this rule, b7 may be considered a chord tone.

This covers several possibilities, including the most common uses of b2 and b6. Other useful applications of this rule will also be shown in the following formulas.

Let's take, for example,
$$\left|\begin{array}{c|c} \text{I} & \text{IV} \\ 5\ b6 & 3\ (6) \end{array}\right|$$

This means that 5 of the I chord and 3 of the IV chord (which would be 6 of the I chord) can be connected with b6 of the I. This particular riff is tricky because it is difficult to hit b6 directly.

The reverse riff-
$$\left|\begin{array}{c|c} \text{IV} & \text{I} \\ 5\ b5 & b7\ (4) \end{array}\right|$$
is much easier (this involves an overblown bent note). Here are more formulas:

$$\left|\begin{array}{cc|cc|cc|cc} \text{I} & \text{IV} & \text{IV} & \text{I} & \text{I} & \text{IV} & \text{IV} & \text{I} \\ b3\ 3 & 1\ (4) & 1\ 7 & b3(b7) & b7\ 7 & 5(8) & 5\ b5 & b7(4) \end{array}\right|$$

$$\left|\begin{array}{cc|cc|cc|cc|cc} \text{I} & \text{V} & \text{V} & \text{I} & \text{IV} & \text{V} & \text{V} & \text{IV} & \text{IV} & \text{V} \\ 1\ b2 & 5(2) & 5b5 & 1(4) & 1\ b2 & 1(2) & 1\ 7 & 1(b7) & 3\ 4 & 3(b5) \end{array}\right|$$

$$\left|\begin{array}{cc|cc|cc|cc|cc} \text{V} & \text{IV} & \text{IV} & \text{V} & \text{V} & \text{IV} & \text{IV} & \text{V} & \text{V} & \text{IV} \\ 3b3 & 3(b2) & 5b6 & 5\ 6 & 5b5 & 5(4) & b7\ 7 & b7(8) & b7\ 6 & b7(b6) \end{array}\right|$$

Not all these formulas are possible on the diatonic harp, but they are useful to know if you have a chromatic harmonica.

Another use of b2 is in ninth chord riffs as a passing tone between 1 and 2 or 2 and 1 (see solo 7, measure 10) or as a lower auxiliary note to 2.(the 9th) In a typical ninth chord riff, the melody will usually go up to 8 and then to 2, or to 2 from a chord tone or b7 and then down to 8. b2 can be used as passing tone in between 8 and 2 in these situations and 2 will usually be the highest note in the riff. b7 2 b7 or 2 b7 2 are possibilities, as well as 2 b2 2 8, 2 8 b2 8, 8 b2 8 2, etc.

● 3. b5 can be used as a passing note in between 5 and 4, or 4 and 5, as a lower neighboring tone in between 5 and its repetition, as an upper neighboring tone in between 4 and its repetition, as part of a connective riff for chord changes, as an appoggiatura to 5, or as a substitute for 5.

b5 is a "blue" note (along with b3 and b7). With the exception of b5 as a substitute for 5, Rule 3 should be easy to understand. The use of b5 as a substitute for 5 is also limited, and mainly applies to sequences like 1 b5 4 b3 1, 8 b5 4 b3 1, etc. Examples of b5 as an appoggiatura to 5 would include sequences such as 1 b5 5, 8 b5 5, b7 b5 5, etc.

● **4**. 7 can be used as an auxiliary note to 8, as a passing tone in between b7 and 8, or 8 and b7. 7 can also preceed 8 if it follows 6. The sequences 5 6 7 8 or 8 7 6 5 are also possible. b7 will sound more bluesy than 7 as a lower auxiliary note to 8 but 7 can also be used. 7 as a passing note between b7 and 8, or 8 and b7 is quite useful. The sequence 5 6 b7 7 8 or its reverse is also possible. 7 in the upper register of the IV chord is also used as a substitute for b7.

At this point, it is possible to connect chord-tones chromatically. Here are some common formulas:

| 1 2 b3 3 | 3 b3 2 1 | b3 4 b5 5 | 5 b5 4 b3 | 3 4 b5 5 | 5 b5 4 b3 |
| 5 6 b7 7 8 | 8 7 b7 6 5 | b3 3 4 b5 5 |

Notice how b2 and b6 are avoided in these sequences. These runs may also be used as three or four note riffs that connect chords. Here are some formulas:

1)	I	IV	2)	I	IV	3)	IV	V	4)	I	V
	12b33	1(4)		1 7	3(6)		34b5	1(5)		34b5	1(5)

5)	V	I	6)	I	IV	7)	V	I
	87b7	b3(b6)		34b5	1(5)		85b6	3(6)

As before, the number in parenthesis indicates what the scale degree would be if the chord had not changed.

Also concerning chord changes, there are some other common ways to use non-chord tones in riffs where the chord changes. The anticipation is sounded as a non-chord tone usually on the fourth off beat, and is held or repeated over the bar line as a chord tone after the change. Anticipations often occur a half beat before the bar line. Here's an example for measures 12-1 of a 12-bar blues. This riff could also be syncopated by tying the anticipation to the repeated note.

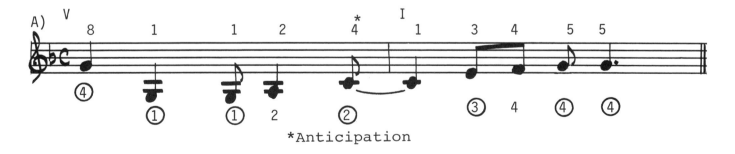

*Anticipation

The suspension is where a chord tone is held over a bar line, where it then becomes a non-chord tone, and then resolves by step to a chord tone of the new chord. Here are some examples:

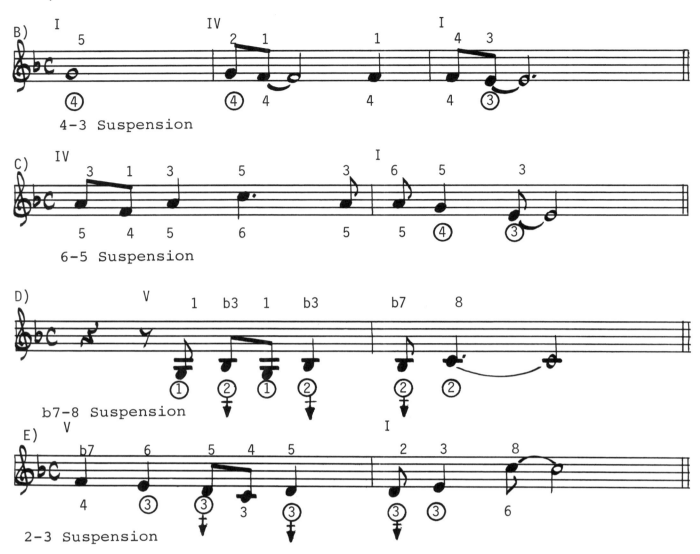

4-3 Suspension

6-5 Suspension

b7-8 Suspension

2-3 Suspension

The **pedal point**, so called because of its use in Baroque organ music, is a chord tone that is held or repeated through a sequence of three or more chords and is part of the first and last chords. A good example of this is a solo Big Walter Horton played one time where he held the fifth of the I chord for the full twelve bars. The fifth is a chord tone of the I & V chords but is a non-chord tone (2) of the IV chord scale.

―――――――Here are some riffs which illustrate―――――――
the uses of b2, b6 b5 and 7.

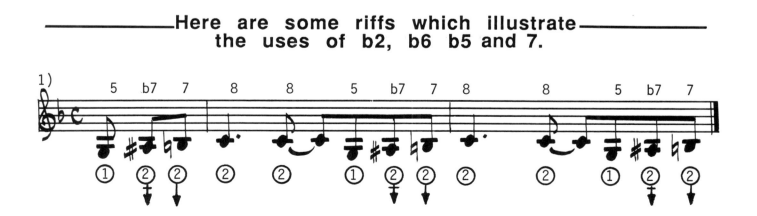

*Don't tongue on repeated note

Solo 13 demonstrates two note riffs. To explain exactly which two-note combinations are possible and which are not would require an explanation of harmony far beyond the scope of this book. Basically, any two chord tones or any chord tone and b7 may be played together. As mentioned before, non-chord tones may be used together as auxiliary or passing chords but this is where complications arise. See solo 13: it does show several of the possibilities.

The next aspect of improvising we need to consider is filling in the gaps between vocal lines of songs. In the blues, the **fills** usually come in the third and fourth, seventh and eighth, and eleventh and twelfth measures and will mostly be I chord riffs (except for measure twelve). This practice of filling in the vocal gaps has it origins in call-and-response work singing where a team leader in a field, for example, would sing a line and the other workers would sing a rejoinder. An example of a blues song, "Easy Rider," with sample fills, has been included.

Easy Rider

VOICE

Traditional

Eas - y rid-er, just see what you have done, 3 ④ 5 ④ 5 ④ ⑤ 5 ③ ③ 6

Eas - y rid-er just see what you have done, ④ ④ 5 ④ ④ 4 ③ ① 2 ② you

made me love you and now your man has come. 6 ⑤ 5 ④ 5 ③ ③ ② 2 ① ②

ADDITIONAL VERSES

2. If I was a catfish, swimming in the deep blue sea (2x)
   I'd swim across the ocean and bring my baby back to me.

3. I'm going away Rider, and I won't be back 'till fall (2x)
   If I find me a woman, I won't be back at all.

When you are playing fills, be tasteful. Let the fills agree with the spirit of the song. You should not try to cram a lot of flash into a song with a slow, graceful melody line, for example.

With soloing, similar considerations apply. A good solo is more than a succession of riffs. The phrases should relate to each other, with the opening riff setting the mood for the solo. There are also extremes which must be avoided. If the phrases are too similar, the solo may sound rigid or dull. If the phrases are too dissimilar, the solo may lack a sense of cohesion or logical continuity. Also, avoid using one rhythm continuously, such as "walking" quarter notes, "running" eighths, continuous triplets, etc. Although this can be done occasionally for effect and is even useful as an exercise, too much quickly becomes monotonous. Rests in particular can be quite effective for developing the necessary rhythmic variety that is essential to good phrasing.

As you study this book, you should listen to recordings the master blues harp players (Little Walter, Big Walter, Sonny Boy Williams II and Paul Butterfield are my personal favorites), learn the solos note for note whenever possible, and analyze them. What you will discover upon analysis of the classic harp solos is that all the great players had a tendency to superimpose I chord riffs over the IV and V chords in order to use the draw reeds to the best advantage. This is particularly true of IV chord riffs, where the only available blue notes in the low register are b5 and b7 . This superimposition of I chord riffs over the IV or V chord could be explained as a kind of bitonality, which is a term describing music simultaneously occurring in two different keys. Personally, I tend to think of it as playing against the chord changes rather than with them.

This book tells you how to play with the chord changes, which is an area where most harp players are deficient, but on the other hand, it is not really wrong to play against the chord changes either. After all, if Little Walter or Paul Butterfield constantly broke all the rules detailed in this chapter, can these rules really be considered binding?

Paul Butterfield

The answer is that if you learn the rules and know how to follow them, you will be free to play with or against the chord changes according to your fancy. If you choose to try a more traditional sounding riff that goes against the changes, and the result doesn't satisfy you, you'll know exactly why. On the other hand, if you want to approach a harp solo in the manner of a guitarist or horn player who knows exactly how to blow smoothly over the chord changes, that option will be open to you.

Gradually, through the process of study, listening, analysis, and experimentation, you will be able to achieve the goal of a convincing blues harp style that is yours alone. Here are some more solos.

Solo 8

This is an example of a close-knit, cohesive solo where the phrases have a strong relationship to each other.

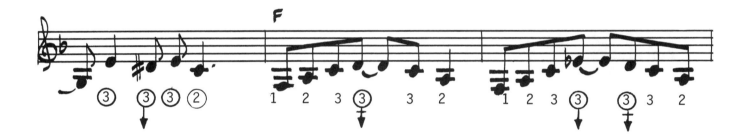

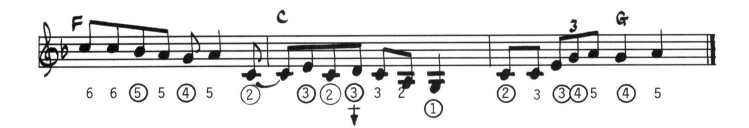

Solo 9

This is a less cohesive solo than Solo 8. Because the opening idea takes place within a narrow range, repeating it in the IV and V chords would be tedious. To avoid this, the solo breaks out of the pattern established in the first four bars, drops into the low register for the IV chord and returns to the middle register.

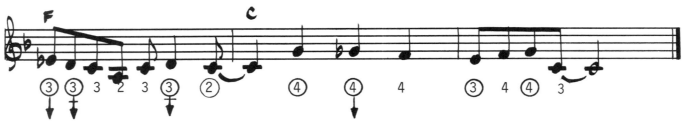

Solo 1 0

This solo has more of rock feel, owing to the straight eighth rhythm and the phrasing. The piece stays closely knit until just before the V chord. Here it changes rhythm to avoid repetition.

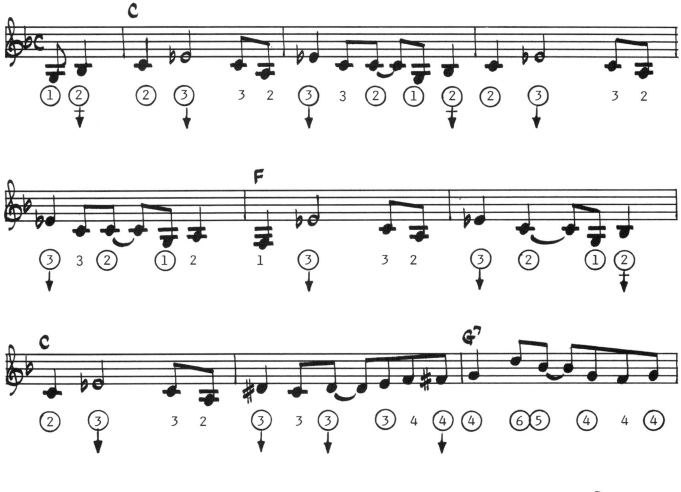

63

Solo 11

This solo jumps quickly into the high register. In the fifth measure, there occurs an overblown bent note on 8-out (b3 of the IV chord). The solo drops back down into the middle, and then the low register in measures 7 and 8. In measure 9, you have a pentatonic major riff which is tricky- it involves jumping from a whole note bend, directly to a half note bend, 5 to 3 in the V chord).

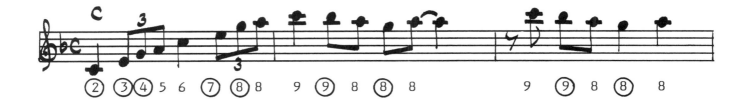

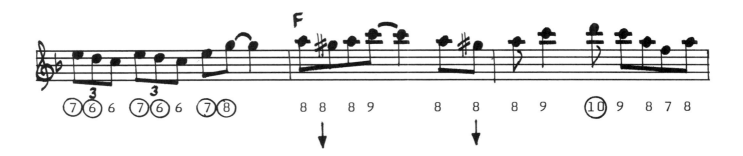

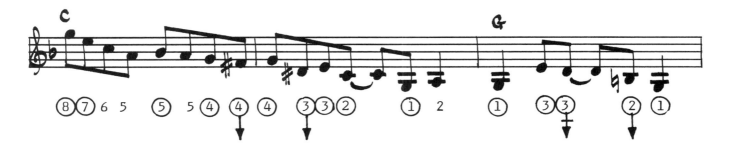

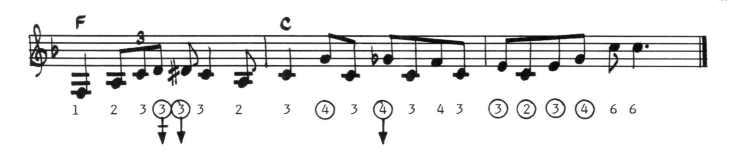

64

Solo 12

This solo maintains an almost continuous running triplet pattern. The walking quarter note rhythm of measures 5 and 9 provides the necessary sharp contrast to the triplets, saving the solo from monotony. This one is a workout!

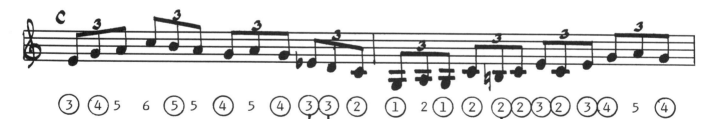

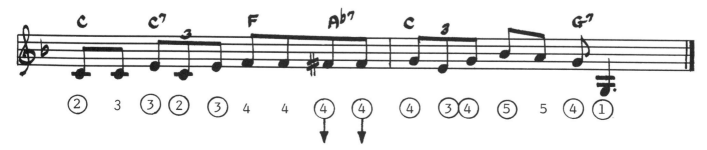

Solo 13

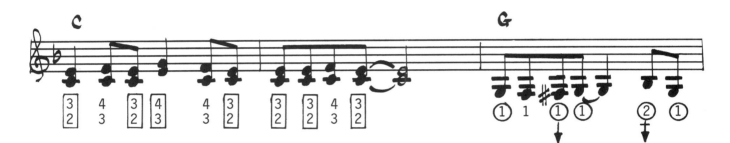

CHAPTER 9

-STRAIGHT HARP-

When the harmonica is played in the tonic key (the key stamped on the harmonica) it is called "straight" harp. Very often, folk, country and even some rock songs will sound better with straight harp than with blues harp. The absence of "blue" notes or funky rhythms in the vocal line is an indication that a song may work better this way.

Table 18   Scale Degrees for Straight Harp

Draw Reeds ○

	1	2	3	4	5	6	7	8	9	10
I	2	5	7	2	4	6	7	2	4	6
1/2 bend	b2	b5	b7	b2	3	b6				
whole bend		4	6							
1 1/2 bend			b6							
IV	6	2	b5	6	1	3	b5	6	1	3
1/2 bend	b6	b2	4	b6	7	b3				
whole bend		1	3							
1 1/2 bend			b3							
V	5	1	3	5	b7	2	3	5	b7	2
1/2 bend	b5	7	b3	b5	6	b2				
whole bend		b7	2							
1 1/2 bend			b2							

Blow Reeds

	1	2	3	4	5	6	7	8	9	10
I	1	3	5	1	3	5	1	3	5	1
1/2 bend							7	b3	b5	7
whole bend								2	4	b7
IV	5	7	2	5	7	2	5	7	2	5
1/2 bend							b5	b7	b2	b5
whole bend								6	1	4
V	4	6	1	4	6	1	4	6	1	4
1/2 bend							3	b6	7	3
whole bend								5	b7	b3

Table 18 is actually Table 17 revised for straight harp. All the improvisational rules still hold, of course, but now your melodic possibilities are different. For the I chord (the IV in blues harp), the "blue" notes are now playable by overblowing rather than overdrawing. In the middle octave of the I chord, pentatonic major riffs will work well. All those funky I chord blues harp riffs can now be used for the V chord. The IV chord is where you will have to learn to find your way around. The sequence exercises in Chapters 6 and 7 can be of some use in learning the new I, IV and V scales. Use IV chord sequences for the I and I chord sequences for the V chord. For the IV chord, try sequence exercises that don't have b3 or b7. Solo 14 is for straight harp and is a boogie-woogie pattern in swing eighths with triplet embellishments.

Solo 14
Straight Harp Shuffle

4 4 5 5 6 6 ⑥ 6 ⑥ 7 7 ⑥ 6 6 6 5 ③ 6 5 4 4 5 5 6 6 ⑥ 6 ⑥

7 ⑥ 6 7 ⑥ 6 5 6 ⑤ ⑤ ⑥ ⑥ 7 7 ⑧ 7 ⑧ ⑨ ⑨ ⑧ ⑧ 7 7 ⑧ 7 ⑥

4 4 5 5 6 6 ⑥ 6 ⑥ 7 7 ⑥ ⑥ 6 6 5 6 5 6 6 ⑦ ⑦ ⑧ ⑧ 8 ⑧ ⑦

⑤ ⑤ ⑥ ⑥ 7 7 ⑧ 7 ⑥ 6 8 6 ⑤ ⑧ ⑤ 5 7 ⑥ 6 7 4

CHAPTER 10

PLAYING IN THE THIRD, FOURTH, FIFTH AND SIXTH POSITIONS

In addition to playing in the tonic (straight harp) and dominant (blues harp) keys, it is also possible to play the blues in what harmonica players call the **higher positions**, which are really the same as modes. Straight harp is called first position and blues harp second position.

When the second degree of the major scale (re) becomes the tonic, it is called the Dorian Mode (See Chapter 5). In blues harp, the Dorian Mode is the V chord scale, but when it is used as the I chord scale it is called third position.

Similarly, the Phrygian mode has the third major scale degree as it's tonic (mi) and is called fourth position. The other two higher positions are the fifth position, which has the sixth degree of the major scale (la) as its tonic and is also known as the Aeolian move or natural minor, and the sixth position, which has the fourth degree of the major scale (fa) as its tonic and is also known as the Lydian move.

A seventh position, with the seventh step of the major scale (ti) as its tonic, known as the Locrian mode, is also possible, but is not used for the same reason that the Locrian mode is excluded from the study of counterpoint - the lack of natural fifth in the scale.

Of all the higher positions, third position is the most widely used, and is therefore the one most worth learning. Solo 15 has been provided to show you some third position riffs.

Solo 15

Scale Degree Charts for Positions 3-6

Table 19 consists of scale degree charts for the four higher positions. To familiarize yourself with the location of the notes try the sequence exercises in Chapters 6 and 7, bending the notes wherever necessary in order to get the correct sequence. Also, take the melodic analysis of any riff or solo in this book, and use the same scale degrees to find it in the other positions. This exercise is called **transposition** and can also be used to learn blues harp riffs on straight harp. With these two exercises as a start, you should be able to work out some riffs and solos in the other positions.

TABLE 19

Third Position-Dorian Mode

DRAW ◯

	1	2	3	4	5	6	7	8	9	10
I	1	4	6	1	b3	5	6	1	b3	5
1/2 bend	7	3	b6	7	2	b5				
whole bend		b3	5							
1 1/2 bend			b5							
IV	5	1	3	5	b7	2	3	5	b7	2
1/2 bend	b5	7	b3	b5	6	b2				
whole bend		b7	2							
1 1/2 bend			b2							
V	4	b7	2	4	b6	1	2	4	b6	1
1/2 bend	3	6	b2	3	5	7				
whole bend		b6	1							
1 1/2 bend			7							

BLOW

	1	2	3	4	5	6	7	8	9	10
I	b7	2	4	b7	2	4	b7	2	4	b7
1/2 bend							6	b2	3	6
whole bend								1	b3	b6
IV	4	6	1	4	6	1	4	6	1	4
1/2 bend							3	b6	7	3
whole bend								5	b7	b3
V	b3	5	b7	b3	5	b7	b3	5	b7	b3
1/2 bend							2	b5	6	2
whole bend								4	b6	b2

Fourth Position-Phrygian Mode

DRAW ○

	1	2	3	4	5	6	7	8	9	10
I	b7	b3	5	b7	b2	4	5	b7	b2	4
1/2 bend	6	2	b5	6	1	3				
whole bend		b2	4							
1 1/2 bend			3							
IV	4	b7	2	4	b6	1	2	4	b6	1
1/2 bend	3	6	b2	3	5	b7				
whole bend		b6	1							
1 1/2 bend			7							
V	b3	b6	1	b3	b5	b7	1	b3	b5	b7
1/2 bend	2	5	7	2	4	6				
whole bend		b5	b7							
1 1/2 bend			6							

BLOW

	1	2	3	4	5	6	7	8	9	10
I	b6	1	b3	b6	1	b3	b6	1	b3	b6
1/2 bend							5	7	2	5
whole bend								b7	b2	b5
IV	b3	5	b7	b3	5	b7	b3	5	b7	b3
1/2 bend							2	b5	6	2
whole bend								4	b6	b2
V	b2	4	b6	b2	4	b6	b2	4	b6	b2
1/2 bend							1	3	5	1
whole bend								b3	b5	7

Fifth Position-Aeolian Mode

DRAW ○

	1	2	3	4	5	6	7	8	9	10
I	4	b7	2	4	b6	1	2	4	b6	1
1/2 bend	3	6	b2	3	5	7				
whole bend		b6	1							
1 1/2 bend			7							
IV	1	4	6	1	b3	5	6	1	b3	5
1/2 bend	7	3	b6	7	2	b5				
whole bend		b3	5							
1 1/2 bend			b5							
V	b7	b3	5	b7	b2	4	5	b7	b2	4
1/2 bend	6	2	b5	6	1	3				
whole bend		b2	4							
1 1/2 bend			3							

71

BLOW

	1	2	3	4	5	6	7	8	9	10
I	b3	5	b7	b3	5	b7	b3	5	b7	b3
1/2 bend							2	b5	6	2
whole bend								4	b6	b2
I V	b7	2	4	b7	2	4	b7	2	4	b7
1/2 bend							6	b2	3	6
whole bend								1	b3	b6
V	b6	1	b3	b6	1	b3	b6	1	b3	b6
1/2 bend							5	7	2	5
whole bend								b7	b2	b5

Sixth Position-Lydian Mode

DRAW ◯

	1	2	3	4	5	6	7	8	9	10
I	6	2	b5	6	1	3	b5	6	1	3
1/2 bend	b6	b2	4	b6	7	b3				
whole bend		1	3							
1 1/2 bend			b3							
I V	3	6	b2	3	5	7	b2	3	5	7
1/2 bend	b3	b6	1	b3	b5	b7				
whole bend		5	7							
1 1/2 bend			b7							
V	2	5	7	2	4	6	7	2	4	6
1/2 bend	b2	b5	b7	b2	3	b6				
whole bend		4	6							
1 1/2 bend			b6							

BLOW

	1	2	3	4	5	6	7	8	9	10
I	5	7	2	5	7	2	5	7	2	5
1/2 bend							b5	b7	b2	b5
whole bend								6	1	4
I V	2	b5	6	2	b5	6	2	b5	6	2
1/2 bend							b2	4	b6	b2
whole bend								3	5	1
V	1	3	5	1	3	5	1	3	5	1
1/2 bend							7	b3	b5	7
whole bend								2	4	b7

CHAPTER 11

TRAIN NOISES,
TRICKS AND SPECIAL TECHNIQUES

We have already talked about the tremelo and the vibrato. In this chapter, I will mention some of the other special effects and tricks harmonica players use. These techniques can spice up your playing considerably.

1. TRAIN NOISES--The harmonica can mimic the sound of a train wonderfully. A solo, "Training Program," (pg. 74) replete with whistle noises and the sound of a train accelerating down the tracks, is included to teach you the ropes of "railroad harmonica." When you get to the triplets that first occur in the fifth and sixth measures, whisper "hoodlely" with each triplet. This will help you get the right tonguing for the triplets. Try using the tremelo on the double note bends (the train whistle). After the train effects, the solo concludes with a rollicking 12-bar blues.

2. TONGUE BLOCKING--This technique is used mainly for straight harp although there are some I or IV chord blues riffs that work out well with it. First, play four reeds at once and then block the lower three with your tongue, leaving the highest note uncovered. Try playing 7-out with 4, 5 and 6 blocked. This technique can also be used in a fast riff that skips over a couple of reeds. For note bending, cover part of the hole you are bending with your tongue.
Tongue blocking is also used for playing a melody line and providing chords below it by uncovering the blocked holes and reblocking them. When this is done, the melody note will always be the highest (or rightmost) note, with the chords on the left. Some country blues players do use this particular technique, but it seems to me to be most useful for folk songs, airs, fiddle tunes and other old-time melodies.

3. OCTAVES--If you use the bottom, that is the underside of the tongue to block two reeds in the middle leaving two reeds unblocked on either side, you can play octaves. Study Table 17 (pg.39) to see which octave combinations are possible and then try working out some riffs with octaves. Another technique done with octaves is alternating between the two reeds on either side of the tongue. Do not move the tongue much for this, just shift it from side to side. This is called the octave tremelo and is used in blues.

4. THE TRILL--This is a rapid alternation between two adjacent reeds--most often ④ and ⑤ . You can do this either by holding the harp with one hand and shaking it back and forth while you draw or blow, or by moving your head instead of your hand. The second method is considered better. The trill can also be combined with note bending.

5. THE GROWL--This trick is hard to describe but the sound it produces is unmistakeable. Basically, the tongue flutters while you inhale. First, say "chutzpah" while breathing in, or fake a snore, being careful not to allow the tongue to touch the back of the throat. Then pick a draw reed and try it. This also works with note bending.

6. THE QUOTE--Not a technique per se, but rather an improvisational device favored by jazz players and done for laughs. Take an uptempo blues solo, and when you have two consecutive measures of the same chord, throw in the first two measures of a tune such as "Jingle Bells," "Dixie," "Turkey in the Straw," a bugle call, etc.. The one qualification is that there should not be a chord change in the first two measures of the tune from which you are quoting otherwise, the quote will not work.

7. THE SLIDE--Start on a low note at least two reeds below the note to which you are going to slide.up to. The lower note should be in the same direction--that is, blow or draw as the high note. Then, as quickly as possible, slide up to the high note by turning your head to the right as your hands move to the left. Known as a melodic ornamentation, and the two or more rapid notes that are created by using this technique are called grace notes. The slide is useful when going to a long note but can be used before an eighth note if the previous note was a long note. Also known as the glissando, the slide can also be used to go down to a low note from a high note.

8. OTHER USES OF TONGUING-- In addition to the two uses of tonguing already described (repeating a note or as a means of preventing one or more reeds from sounding when changing rapidly in between two non-adjacent reeds), tonguing can also be used at other times to give a riff a more percussive or staccato sound. (Lagato is a smooth, continuous flow of notes-staccato is best described through comparison to machine gunfire.) Try experimenting with this technique to see where it will sound good. First if you are playing quarter notes on adjacent in or out reeds, it is not always necessary to slur the notes (slurring is connecting the notes with the same breath). Instead, you can get a more marked quality to the notes by stopping the breath without tonguing. A riff can be made to sound more percussive this way as well as by tonguing.

9. NOSE HARP--Yes, folks, you can play it with your nose! Cover one nostril with a finger, press the harp against your other nostril, and play. This one is always good for a laugh and is a great way to impress someone who you would like to get to know a little better. Be careful to avoid sneezing while playing nose harp, however, lest the draw reeds aquire an unpleasant taste.

By the way, I heard an amusing anecdote, narrated by a superb harmonicist named Mark Graham, about an old-timer who could at the same time play one harp with his mouth and one harp with his nose! Later on, I read that Sonny Boy Williamson II (Rice Miller) could do the same thing.

Solo 16
Training Program

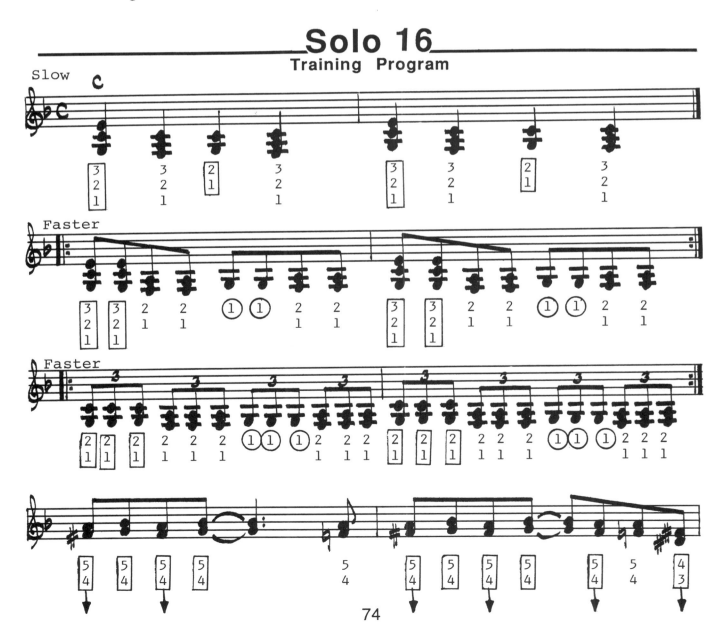

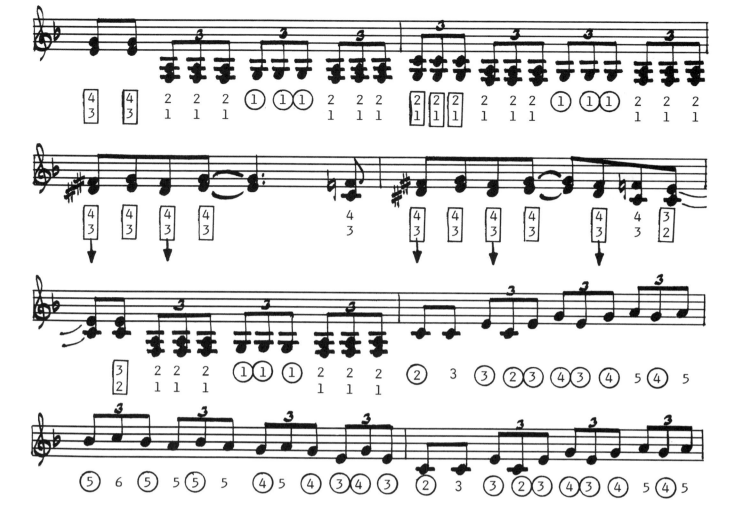

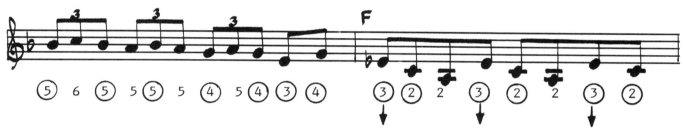

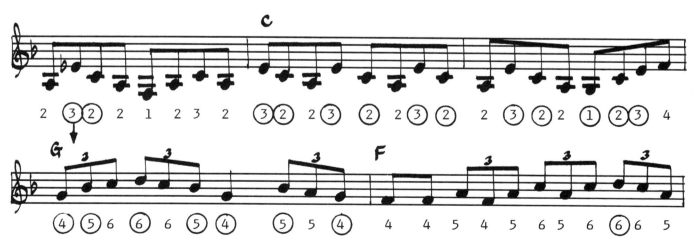

CHAPTER 12

-PLAYING ROCK-

Rock, like jazz, grew out of the blues and many famous rock songs are, in fact, 12-bar blues. Other rock songs consist of the I, IV and V chords in different sequences. (Most songs other than blues start on the I chord, end on I, progress to the V chord at the halfway point of the verse or chorus and have a V chord before the closing I chord).

Still, other songs will use minor chords and other kinds of chords that may be new to you. The rhythms in rock songs can also be different from the swing eighth rhythm that predominates the blues, but a new rhythm is something you can feel and pick up easily if your ear is good enough.

You'll need to expand your musical horizons in regards to chords. Playing rock will require you to play over several different chords and the information you will need is given in Table 20.

KEYS

TABLE 20

Chords	Scale Degrees	A	B	C	D	E	F	G
I	1 3 5	A	B	C-CEG	D	E	F	G
II	2 4 6	Bm	C#m	Dm-DFA	Em	F#m	Gm	Am
III	3 5 7	C#m	D#m	Em-EGB	F#m	G#m	Am	Bm
IV	4 6 1	D	E	F-FAC	G	A	Bb	C
V(7)	5 7 2 (4)	E7	F#	G7-GBDF	A(7)	B(7)	C(7)	D(7)
VI	6 1 3	F#m	G#m	Am-ACE	Bm	C#m	Dm	Em
VII	7 2 4	G#dim	A#dim	Bdim-BDF	C#dim	D#dim	Edim	F#dim
V7ofII	6 b2 3 5	F#7	G#7	A7-AC#EG	B7	C#7	D7	E7
V7ofIII	7b3b56	G#7	A#7	B7-BD#F#A	C#7	D#7	E7	F#7
V7of IV	1 3 5 b7	A7	B7	C7-CEGBb	D7	E7	F7	G7
V7 of V	2 b5 6 1	B7	C#7	D7-DF#AC	E7	F#7	G7	A7
V7of VI	3 b6 7 2	C#7	D#7	E7-EG#BD	F#7	G#7	A7	B7
bIIImaj.	b3 5 b7	C	D	Eb-EbGBb	F	G	Ab	Bb
bVImaj.	b6 1 b3	F	G	Ab-AbCEb	Bb	C	Db	Eb
IVminor	4 b6 1	Dm	Em	Fm-FAbC	Gm	Am	Bbm	Cm
IV of IV	b7 2 4	G	A	Bb-BbDF	C	D	Eb	F

Table 20 gives 16 of the most commonly used chords in the seven keys most often used in rock, and also tells you the scale degrees in each of these chords. The names of the notes of the chords have been given for the key of C as an example.

Reading down the column on the far left-hand side, you will see the first seven chords in Roman numerals I through VII. These are the diatonic chords, the chords which have only notes that can be found in the major scale. I, IV and V are major, II, III and VI are minor and VII is diminished (1b3b5 is the formula for a diminished triad).

Next to V, there is an Arabic seven in parenthesis. This means that the flat b7 (the fourth tone of the major scale) can be added to the chord. V7 is frequently substituted for V.

The next five chords in the far left column, V7 of II, V7 of III, V7 of IV, V7 of V and V7 of VI, are called secondary dominants. A secondary dominant is a dominant seventh chord (1 #3 5 b7) built on the note five steps up from the chord to which it is in dominant relationship. For example, in the key of C the note A is five steps up from the note D, so A7 would be the secondary dominant of Dm. The secondary dominant usually goes to the chord five steps down (A7-Dm), although there are exceptions (V7 of VI-IV). Secondary dominants can also occur as major chords rather than sevenths.

The next two chords are bIII major and bVI major, which are major chords built on the notes b3 and b6 of the major scale, respectively. The last two chords are the minor form of the IV chord, IV minor (which often follows IV), and the IV of IV chord, which might also be described as bVII major. The IV of IV is technically known as a secondary subdominant-- that is, a chord built on a note four steps up the scale from the chord to which it is in subdominant relationship.

In the column marked "Scale Degrees," the notes that make up each chord are given in the order of the tonic, third, fifth and flat seventh, if the chord is a seventh chord. Some of these notes are only playable by directly hitting a bent note. You may have to avoid b6 altogether and use riffs not involving it, or only use it after 6.

Kit Gamble

77

-STRIGHT HARP-

TABLE 21

chords with roots on:

IN ○	1	2	3	4	5	6	7	8	9	10
I	2	5	7	2	4	6	7	2	4	6
	b2	b5	b7	b2	3	b6				
		4	6							
			b6							
bII	b2	b5	b7	b2	3	b6	b7	b2	3	b6
	b4	4	6	1	b3	5				
		3	b6							
			5							
II	1	4	6	1	b3	5	6	1	b3	5
	7	3	b6	7	2	b5				
		b3	5							
			b5							
bIII	7	3	b6	7	2	b5	b6	7	2	b5
	b7	b3	5	b7	b2	4				
		2	5							
			4							
III	b7	b3	5	b7	b2	4	5	b7	b2	4
	6	2	b5	6	1	3				
		b2	4							
			3							
IV	6	2	b5	6	1	3	b5	6	1	3
	b6	b2	4	b6	7	b3				
		1	3							
			b3							
bV	b6	b2	4	b6	7	b3	4	b6	7	b3
	5	1	3	5	b7	2				
		7	b3							
			2							
V	5	1	3	5	b7	2	3	5	b7	2
	b5	7	b3	b5	6	b2				
		b7	2							
			b2							
bVI	b5	7	b3	b5	6	b2	b3	b5	6	b2
	4	b7	2	4	b6	1				
		6	b2							
			1							
VI	4	b7	2	4	b6	1	2	4	b6	1
	3	6	b2	3	5	7				
		b6	1							
			7							
bVII	3	6	b2	3	5	7	b2	3	5	7
	b3	b6	1	b3	b5	b7				
		5	7							
			b7							
VII	b3	b6	1	b3	b5	b7	1	b3	b5	b7
	2	5	7	2	4	6				
		b5	b7							
			6							

chords with roots on:

OUT	1	2	3	4	5	6	7	8	9	10
I	1	3	5	1	3	5	1	3	5	1
							7	b3	b5	7
								2	4	b7
bII	7	b3	b5	7	b3	b5	7	b3	b5	7
							b7	2	4	6
								b2	3	b6
II	b7	2	4	b7	2	4	b7	2	4	b7
							6	b2	3	6
								1	b3	b6
bIII	6	b2	3	6	b2	3	6	b2	3	6
							b6	1	b3	b6
								7	2	5
III	b6	1	b3	b6	1	b3	b6	7	b3	b6
							5	b7	2	5
								6	b2	b5
IV	5	7	2	5	7	2	5	7	2	5
							b5	b7	b2	b5
								6	1	4
bV	b5	b7	b2	b5	b7	b2	b5	b7	b2	b5
							4	6	1	4
								b6	7	3
V	4	6	1	4	6	1	4	6	1	4
							3	b6	7	3
								5	b7	b3
bVI	3	b6	7	3	b6	7	3	b6	7	3
							b3	5	b7	b3
								b5	6	2
VI	b3	5	b7	b3	5	b7	b3	5	b7	b3
							2	b5	6	2
								4	b6	b2
bVII	2	b5	6	2	b5	6	2	b5	6	2
							b2	4	b6	b2
								3	5	1
VII	b2	4	b6	b2	4	b6	b2	4	b6	b2
							1	3	5	1
								b3	b5	7

SCALE DEGREE CHART FOR ALL ROOT NOTES
-BLUES HARP-

chords with roots on:

OUT	1	2	3	4	5	6	7	8	9	10
I	4	6	1	4	6	1	4	6	1	4
							3	b6	7	3
								5	b7	b3
bII	3	b6	7	3	b6	7	3	b6	7	3
							b3	5	b7	b3
								b5	6	2
II	b3	5	b7	b3	5	b7	b3	5	b7	b3
							2	b5	6	2
								4	b6	b2
bIII	2	b5	6	2	b5	6	2	b5	6	2
							b2	4	b6	b2
								3	5	1
III	b2	4	b6	b2	4	b6	b2	4	b6	b2
							1	3	5	1
								b3	b5	7
IV	1	3	5	1	3	5	1	3	5	1
							7	b3	b5	7
								2	4	b7
bV	7	b3	b5	7	b3	b5	7	b3	b5	7
							b7	2	4	b7
								b2	3	6
V	b7	2	4	b7	2	4	b7	2	4	b7
							6	b2	3	6
								1	b3	b6
bVI	6	b2	3	6	b2	3	6	b2	3	6
							b6	1	b3	b6
								7	2	5
VI	b6	1	b3	b6	1	b3	b6	1	b3	b6
							5	7	2	5
								b7	b2	b5
VII	5	7	2	5	7	2	5	7	2	5
							b5	b7	b2	b5
								6	1	4
bVII	b5	b7	b2	b5	b7	b2	b5	b7	b2	b5
							4	6	1	4
								b6	7	3

Table 21 is a complete scale degree chart for all root note positions, written out for both blues and straight harp. The previous scale degree charts were all designed for the I, IV and V chords only, which was sufficient for 12-bar blues. Table 21, on the other hand, gives you the location of the scale degrees as counted from each of the twelve tones of the chromatic scale, therefore enabling you to play over all the chords listed in Table 20. Some of these chords will be easier to play over than others, depending on what kind of note bending is required. Sometimes you might have to hold a long note on a chord tone just to be melodicly correct in a difficult situation.

-BLUES HARP-

chords with roots on:

roots	IN○	1	2	3	4	5	6	7	8	9	10
I		5	1	3	5	b7	2	3	5	b7	2
		b5	7	b3	b5	6	b2				
			b7	2							
				b2							
bII		b5	7	b3	b5	6	b2	b3	b5	6	b2
		4	b7	2	4	b6	1				
			6	b2							
				1							
II		4	b7	2	4	b6	1	2	4	b6	1
		3	6	2	3	5	7				
			b6	1							
				7							
bIII		3	6	b2	3	5	7	b2	3	5	7
		b3	6	1	b3	b5	b7				
			5	7							
				b7							
III		b3	b6	1	b3	b5	b7	1	b3	b5	b7
		2	5	7	2	4	6				
			b5	b7							
				6							
IV		2	5	7	2	4	6	7	2	4	6
		b2	b5	b7	b2	3	b6				
			4	6							
				b6							
bV		b2	b5	b7	b2	3	b6	b7	b2	3	b6
		1	4	6	1	b3	5				
			3	b6							
				5							
V		1	4	6	1	b3	5	6	1	b3	5
		7	3	b6	7	2	b5				
			b3	5							
				b5							
bVI		7	b3	b6	7	2	b5	b6	7	2	b5
		b7	3	5	b7	b2	4				
			2	b5							
				4							
VI		b7	b3	5	b7	b2	4	5	b7	b2	4
		6	2	b5	6	1	3				
			b2	4							
				3							
bVII		6	2	b5	6	1	3	b5	6	1	3
		b6	b2	4	b6	7	b3				
			1	3							
				b3							
VII		b6	b2	4	b6	7	b3	4	b6	7	b3
		5	1	3	5	b7	2				
			7	b3							
				2							

Table 21 is intended primarily for reference rather than memorization. It would probably take quite a while to really know it thoroughly, but theoretically you could even use it to play music as complex as bebop jazz (although the chromatic harmonica is undoubtly better for such an undertaking).

When using tables 20 and 21, follow the rules of improvisation as described in Chapter 8, but with two considerations which apply only to the minor chords. **1)** Do not use 3 when you are playing over a minor chord, but always use b3 instead, and. **2)** You can use b6 (that is, the note a half step above the fifth of any chord) as an upper auxiliary note to 5 or as a passing tone. The sequences 5 b6 b7 8, or its reverse, 5 b6 7 8, or its reverse, or even 5 6 7 8 but not its reverse, among others can be used with minor chords. Also, b7 is better than 6 as a single passing tone between 5 and 8 or 8 and 5 when playing over a minor chord.

When you are learning a new song, first memorize the chord sequence and then analyze it using Table 20. If the song is in the key of C and the first four chords are C, Dm, G7, Am, the sequence is I-II-V7-VI. Look up the chord tones for each chord in the column which lists the scale degrees, and then refer to table 21 in order to find the location of non-chord tones.

As starting point, try playing the vocal line. Next, you might try playing the vocal line, embellishing it with some extra notes thrown in here and there. After that, analyze the vocal line and try using different notes than those of the vocal line but with similar rhythms.

This last approach would be basically a harmony part to the vocal line. If you are working out a harmony part, try to stay either above or below the vocal line without crossing it.

The last possibility is to use both different chord tones and different rhythms than those of the vocal line. Any solo played over the chords to a song would tend to fall into one of these four categories, although a combined approach is also possible.

After you have gotten accustomed to playing over rock chord changes using either blues or straight harp, try experimenting with the higher positions for rock playing. Use the I chord rows of the scale degree charts of Table 19 when you are learning where the tones of the various chords are located, and use Table 13 to locate the non-chord tones.

Tom Ball

82

The Minor Key

Many rock songs are written in the minor key. The natural minor scale, (or Aeolian mode) is based on the sixth step of the major scale and shares the same key signature as the major key. Every major key will have a relative minor key. (For example, D minor is the relative minor of F major, the key signature used in this book.) The order of scale degrees for the natural minor is 1, 2, b3, 5, b6, b7, 8. However, when the seventh step of the natural minor scale is raised to 7, it is termed the harmonic minor scale, which is the basis for building chords in the minor key. In the minor key, both the I and IV chords are minor and the B chord is major. If you look at Table 20, you can figure out the chords to the minor key by using VI as the I chord, II as the IV chord, and V7 of V1 as the V chord. For example, A minor is the relative minor of C major and the I, IV and V chords of A minor are A minor, D minor and E major. E7 can be substituted for E major.

The diatonic harmonica was originally designed for major key playing and also works well for modal playing. (You will recall that blues harp or second position is the same as the Mixolydian mode). However, the minor key is somewhat of a problem for the harmonica, because the harmonic minor scale with its raised seventh tone is not considered diatonic (the major scale and the modes are considered diatonic), The difficulty revolves around the fact the the 3 of the V chord in the minor key is the same note as b6 in the major scale and can only be played by note bending.

For playing in the minor key, there are three main approaches, the first two being the use of either the Dorian mode (third position) or the Aeolian mode (fifth position). If you are using the Dorian mode, remember to bend 3-draw down a half step when playing over the minor IV chord, to avoid playing a natural 3 over the b3 in the accompaniment. In both positions, natural 3 of the V chord has to be played by hitting a bent note directly.

The third approach to playing in the minor key is to by a minor key harmonica.

Solo 17

This solo uses a rock rhythm. Straight eighths and sixteenths combine to produce a funky groove.. The trill occurs in the ninth measure and is indicated by the wavy lline.

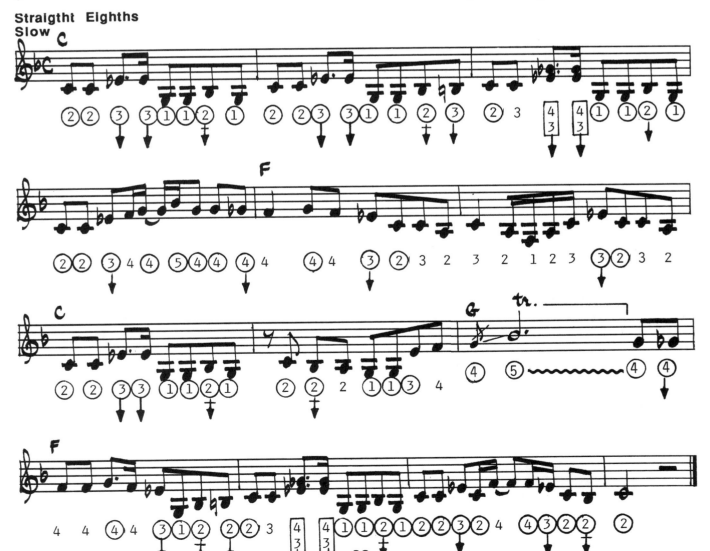

Here's a song that originated in the bluegrass repertory and was later popularized by The Grateful Dead. Entitled *"Goin' Down The Road Feelin' Bad"*, the version here consists of the vocal line, additional verses, and two breaks. The first break bears a resemblance to the vocal line, but the second break while staying within the melodic boundaries imposed by the chord changes, is instead a free-form excursion into bluegrass-style running eighth notes. In the twelfth measure you'll see an A minor chord, which is the VI chord in the key of C. This is the only appearance of a chord other than I, IV or V in this book.

Goin' Down The Road Feelin' Bad

84

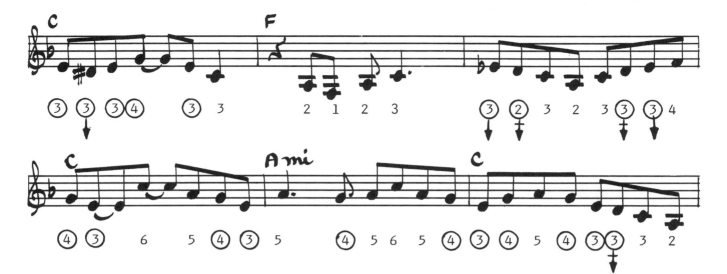

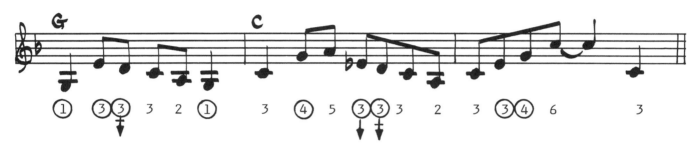

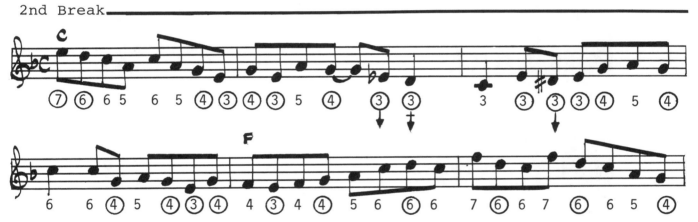

2nd Break _____

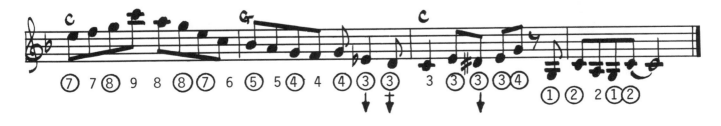

Goin' where the water tastes like wine. (3x)
Ain't gonna be treated this-away.

Goin' where the climate suits my clothes. (3x)
Ain't gonna be treaded this-away.

I'm down in that jailhouse on my knees, (3x)
Ain't gonna be treated this-away.

Norton Buffalo

CHAPTER 13

-JAMMING WITH OTHER MUSICIANS-

Eventually, you will want to start jamming with other musicians. By the time you have mastered all the techniques, information, exercises, riffs and solos in this book, you should be a downright dangerous harp player, worthy of any good band. As a start, find yourself a guitarist to jam with. If he does not know how to play 12-bar blues, refer him to Tables 2 and 3 in Chapter 4.

Unless your guitarist is a diehard blues fanatic, he will probably want to do other songs besides 12-bar blues. When this happens, find out the chords. If the song uses chords other than I, IV or V, refer to Table 20 and look up the scale degrees of the other chords. Most country or bluegrass songs, for example, use relatively easy chords.

The real test of your musical ear comes when you are trying to jam to a song and you know the key but not the chords (In musician's parlance this is known as "winging it"). Assuming that you are playing in the dominant key (blues harp), the best approach is to play simple patterns in the lower six reeds, emphasizing the draw notes. This approach, in essence, sticks to I chord riffs and uses a trial-and-error process to see which riffs work with the chord changes. You might want to start with a long ④, which will work with either I, IV or V, and then maybe 3-out. 5-draw requires caution as a long note on ⑤ will conflict with the IV chord. Other than ⑤, all the lower six draw reeds will be serviceable. Use the blow notes as passing or auxiliary tones (except 3-out and 6-out which will be okay as a long note). Try bending notes. Does the note bend fit in? With repeated practice, you will eventually be able to tell if a note jives with the chord or not. To develop your ear, try these tips. First, try playing with records. If you have found a guitarist, ask him what keys your favorite songs are in. (You can also check out a music store and try to locate the appropriate songbooks). Select the correct harp, drop the needle in the groove, and try out some riffs.

Try memorizing and learn to sing all the riffs and solos in this book. Being able to sing anything you can play proves you really know it. In classical music conservatories strong emphasis is placed on singing, even for instrumentalists who have no aspirations as vocalists, because the value of singing as a means of ear training is so well understood. Eventually, you can even study Chapter 8 and sing improvised riffs as well as play them.

Playing in a group situation, you may have to deal with some challenging interpersonal dynamics-namely, musicians who tend to monopolize the breaks. Frank Zappa once termed jam sessions as "exercises in egomania" and it is all to often the case. By the same token, make sure you are not guilty of the same mistake. Always hold back during the vocals or another musician's solo, and wait your turn to take the lead. I usually stick to long notes or percussive riffs in the low reeds when playing back-up.

You may even want to go electric and join a band, for which you will need some sound equipment (no pun intended). For blues playing, use a Shure Green Bullet microphone or some equivalent thereof through an old Fender tube amp (the tweed amps are considered the best for this; the old blackface models are also quite good). The amplifier is in turn miked through a P.A. system.

Other styles such as country, a "cleaner" sound is usually more appropriate. Try a standard vocal mike (the Shure SM-58 is a good bet) plugged directly into the soundboard. Some blues players occasionally prefer the clean sound, particularly with the E and F scale harps. Switching from the "dirty" to the "clean" sound can also create more variety on stage.

One difference between playing amplified with the microphone cupped by the hands and playing without a mike is that it is important to have a good vibrato playing through a mike. Tremelo is generally suited to the clean acoustic sound, and although vibrato can be used for either acoustic or amplified playing, it is more effective with a microphone than the tremelo.

Who knows? Maybe as a result of studying this book, you will become a world-class harmonicist, crowned with fame and fortune. Limosines, the limelight, irresistible sex appeal, a star on your dressing room door--they could all be yours. If and when it does happen, just remember who you could never have done it all without, and be sure to plug this book at every available opportunity!

All kidding aside, it suddenly occurs to me that I have neglected to mention the single most important thing about playing blues harp and in fact about playing music in general - the emotional aspect of creative expression. This was brought home to me in a conversation I had with the great blues harmonicist Junior Wells.

When I was completing the manuscript of this book, Junior Wells and his band came to a nightclub in Albany, NY, my hometown, and played and sang superbly, he made his way through the crowd to the bar, have a drink and mingle with the audience. I approached him and engaged him in conversation. The gist of it was this:

I asked him if he could read music, and he said yes, but only slowly.

When asked if he knew music theory in terms of knowing the I, IV, and V chords, how to count the steps of the scale, etc., he said no, and moreover reacted negatively to the idea. He claimed that too much emphasis on theory would impede the free flow of feeling. He told me emphatically that the feeling was the most vital element in music.

He was right about feeling - no doubt about it, which is why I have saved this point for last. But in defense of the methodology of this book, it must be noted that there have been many fine musicians who improvised blues, rock or jazz from the vantage point of understanding music theory, and have done so with admirable feeling. Will Scarlett, who plays with Hot Tuna, is an example of a harp player who has a good grasp of theory.

Therefore, I can't agree with his disparaging outlook on a theory-based approach to blues harp. Whether he knew it or not (actually his ear knew but his brain didn't) he was following the rules outlined in Chapter Eight of this book. As he played, I listened carefully and could hear the riffs changing appropriately to suit each of the three basic chords of the blues. What made his playing great was his precise timing and superb phrasing (this is where listening to recordings of the blues harp greats comes in - you need this to get the right phrasing).

Although what Junior told me about feeling is the last word on blues harp, you may be curious about some of the other points our conversation touched on.

I told him that I play the harmonica.

"You play harp? You got it on you? You aint no harp player unless you got it on you all the time! Even if you go to the bathroom you gotta have it on you,. Where is it? Let's see it!", Junior demanded.

I showed him a G scale Hohner Blues Harp.

"That aint no good!"

I asked him what he played and he replied that he used Marine Bands and Lee Oskars. He praised the Lee Oskar in particular by the use of an all-purpose obscenity that describes a person who engages in Oedipal behavior.

"You think a Marine Band is better than a Blues Harp?" I asked.

"I know it is", said Junior, who then proceeded to denounce the Blues Harp as an inferior product designed to make kids think they were playing blues, just because it was called a Blues Harp.

I asked him who his favorite harp players are.

He nodded in acknowledgment to the question and held up three fingers of his right hand, saying "Three". He named Sonny Boy Williamson I, Little Walter, and Sonny Boy Williamson II (Rice Miller), adding that Little Walter was the most technically proficient.

I asked him how he learned and he said that each of these three men had spent time with him showing him how to play. He also added that his mother knew the blues pianist Sunnyland Slim when she was pregnant with him, and that Sunnyland Slim had predicted that her child would be a great blues musician.

I then confided to him an idea for a possible future book on blues harp.

He objected at first, accusing me of profiteering motives, to which I responded that helping people learn blues harp was in fact my true motive. He then admitted that I had a good idea, and after the final set came back to me, shook my hand, and told me once again that I had a good idea.

What is it? You'll just have to wait and see.

In the meantime, this book will hopefully provide you with many fruitful hours of study and fun.

Peace,
Glenn Weiser

1. Sonny Boy Williamson I (John Lee Williamson) -
Vol 1-3, Blues Classics #3, #20, & #24
Sonny Boy I pioneered the Chicago blues style and along with Walter Jacobs, Walter Horton and Sonny Boy II (Rice Miller) is considered one of the four greatest Chicago harmonicists.

2. Muddy Waters -
Best of Muddy Waters -Chess CH 9255
Rolling Stone -Chess CH 9101
The Real Folk Blues -Chess CH 9274
I'm Ready-Blue Sky P2-34928
Muddly Waters created and defined the sound of the postwar Chicago blues, and his bands always featured a harp player. The above titles feature the playing of Little Walter, Big Walter, James Cotton, and Jerry Portnoy.

3. Little Walter Jacobs -
The Best of Little Walter Vol. II-Chess CH-9292
Boss Blues Harmonica -Chess CH - 2 - 9209
Confessing The Blues (Import) Chess BRP-2025
The Blues World of Little Walter -Delmark DL-648
Little Walter was Muddy Water's original harmonicist, and was the first to use amplified harmonica. His sound was influenced by the blues sax players (notably Louis Jordan) of his day and was also marked by a strong vibrato. After the success of his hit single, "Juke" he left Muddy to form his own group. Eventually he deteriorated into heavy drinking and was mortally wounded in a Chicago street fight in 1968. He was 37 years old when he died. Incidentally, Little Walter and I share the same birthday - May 1st.

4. Sonny Boy Williamson II (Rice Miller) -
King Biscuit Time -Arhoolie 2020
One Way Out -Chess CH 9116
Down and Out Blues -Chess CH 9257
The Real Folk blues -Chess CH 9272
More Real Folk Blues -Chess CH 9277
Sonny Boy II had a style which I like to compare to Count Basie's jazz piano playing--sparse and impeccably timed. He used the tremelo to great effect and sang in a trembling voice. He claimed to be the original Sonny Boy Williamson ("There ain't no other"), an implausible contention probably born of a quirk in his personality. Sonny Boy Toured Europe in 1964 and died in 1965 at a ripe old age.

5. Big Walter Horton -
The Soul of the blues Harmonica -Chess CH 9268
Fine Cuts -Blind Pig BP 678
Johnny Young and Big Walter - Chicago Blues Arhoolie F-1037
Can' t keep Lovin' You - Blind Pig BP 1484
Big Walter Horton - Alligator 4702
Big Walter Horton - Blueprint BRP - 5150
I Am The Blues (Willie Dixon) -Columbia PC 9987
Big Walter, like Walter Jacobs and Sonny I, started playing when he was very young and played with The Memphis Jug Band in the 1920's. He gave pointers to both Little Walter and Sonny Boy II. Big Walter probably had the best tone of any blues harmonicist before or since; the sounds he could elicit from a Hohner Marine Band still amaze me. Invariably described as shy and nervous, he was more comfortable in the role of a sideman than a bandleader and although he recorded extensively, he never got the recognition he deserved. Big Walter lived a long life and died in 1981.

6. Sonny Terry -
You Hear Me Talkin' -MUSE MR 5131
Sonny Is King! -Bluesville OBC 521
Whoopin' -Alligator 4734
Sonny Terry was from Georgia. Blinded in youth, he turned to the harmonica for solace after the loss of his sight. The quintessential country blues harpman, his style was a lot folkier than his counterparts in Chicago. For years he played as duo act with guitarist/singer Brownie McGhee.

7. Junior Wells -
Hoodoo Man Blues -Delmark DS 612
Blues Hit Big Town -Delmark DL 640
Southside Blues Jam -Delmark DL 628
It's My Life Vanguard -VMS 73120
Junior Wells played with Muddy Waters in the 1950's, and eventually formed a partnership with guitarist Buddy Guy. My meeting with Junior is described in the last chapter of this book.

8. James Cotton -
The Blues Never Die! (Otis Spann) -Prestige PR 7710
Live at Antone's -Antone's Records ANT 0007
Live at Newport (Muddy Waters) -Chess CH 9198
Muddy Waters Sings Big Bill Broonzy -Chess Ch 9197
James Cotton was determined to learn blues harp as a boy and at age nine ran away from home to meet Sonny Boy Williamson II. He told Sonny Boy that he was an orphan, and so Sonny Boy raised him and taught him the harp. Cotton's style is marked by long, expressive wails and a fine tone. He was Muddy's harp player on several of his albums.

9. Paul Butterffield -
The Paul Butterfield Blues Band - Edsel ED 150
East West -Elektra EKS 7315
It All Comes Back -Rhino RNLP 7078
Golden Butter -Elektra 7E-2005
The Butterfield Blues Band/live -Elektra 7E-2001
Better Days -Rhino RNLP 70877
Fathers and Sons -Chess CH2 92522 (Muddy Waters)
Paul Butterfield was a classical flautist prior to taking up the harmonica. He learned directly from the Chicago harp masters and developed a jazzy brand of playing characterized by a greater rhythmic complexity than his predecessors. He did much to popularize the harmonica and played at Woodstock in 1969, where I saw him for a few semiconscious moments. Butterfield ranks with the greatest harpmen and his untimely death in 1987 was greatly lamented.

10. Charlie Musselwhite -
Taking My Time -Arhoolie 1065
Goin' Back Down South -Arhoolie 1074
Charlie Musselwhite, like Paul Butterfield, learned harp from the Chicago greats and made a series of now out of print records on Vanguard ("Stand Back!" is worth looking for).

11. Miscellaneous Harmonicists -

(The following is a list of records containing good harp work. If a record was not made in the harmonicist's name, he will be identified in parenthesis.)

Hot Tuna (Will Scarlett) -RCA AYL 1-3864
Hooker N' Heat (Al Wilson) -Rhino RNDA - 71105
Seigal-Schwall Reunion Concert (Corky Seigal) -Alligator AL-4760
Best of Jimmy Reed -Kent KST - 537
Moanin' in the Moonlight Howlin Wolf -Chess CH - 9195
The James Harman Band Extra Napkins -Reviera RR 505
Little Charlie and The Nightcats -All The Way -Crazy Alligator AL 4753
Disturbing The Peace -Alligator AL 4761
The Fabulous Thunderbirds (Kim Wilson) T-Bird Rhythm -Chrysallis PV 41935
Little Sonny - New King of the Blues Harmonica -Stax MPS 8533
Cary Bell's Blues Harp -Delmark DS 622
Lazy Lester Rides Again -Kingsnake KS 007
Treat Her Right (Jim Fitting) -RCA 6884-1-R
Willie Dixon - Hidden Charms (Sugar Blue) -Capitol C 1 90595
Mickey Raphael - Hand To Mouth -Intercon PCD 85703
Lee Oskar - Introducing Beautiful Melodies
Norton Buffalo - Lovin InThe Valley Of The Moon,1977 -Capitol
　　　　　　　　Desert Horzions,1978 - Capitol
　　　　　　　　Steve Miller Band, Live ,1983 - Capitol

12. Anthologies -

Sun Records Harmonica Classics -Rounder SS-29
Low Blows: An Anthology of Chicago Harmonica -Blues Rooster Blues R7610
Great Harp Players (1927-30) -Matchbox MSE-209
Johnny Young and His Friends -Testament 2226
Wizards From The Southside -Chess CH-9102
An Offer You Can't Refuse (Paul Butterfield & Walter Horton) -Red Lightnin' R008
Chicago Blues - The Early 1950's -Blues Classics BC8

Kellie Rucker

OTHER HARMONICA BOOKS FROM

CENTERSTREAM Publishing, P.O. Box 17878 - Anaheim Hills, CA 92807
Phone/fax (714) 779-9390

Blues & Rock Harmonica
by Glenn Weiser
This book/cassette package helps beginners learn blues & rock improvisation. Includes explanations of scales, modes, chords, and other essential elements of music. The cassette features riffs & solos, plus demonstrations and a blues jam to play along with.
00000127..$18.95

Blues Harmonica – A Comprehensive Crash Course & Overview
by Tom Ball
This new book/cassette pack features a comprehensive crash-course on all aspects of the blues harmonica. Written informally and in only tab notation, this book encourages players to learn at their own pace while developing their own style and feel. The accompanying tape includes demonstrations to inspire and aid players in practice.
00000159..$16.95

The Harmonica According To Charlie Musselwhite
Centerstream Publications
An easy guide to playing improvised blues. Includes a 20 minute record.
_____00000001 ....$8.95

A Sourcebook Of Sonny Terry Licks
for Blues Harmonica
by Tom Ball
Centerstream Publishing
Besides 70 famous licks from Sonny, this book/CD pack gives you some quick harmonica lessons, information on Sonny's style, a discography with key chart, and a bibliography for future research. The CD features each lick played out by the author.
_____00000178 Book/CD Pack $19.95

Fiddletunes For Harmonica
by Glenn Weiser
This complete guide to playing fiddle tunes contains tips on hand positions, playing instructions, and techniques, plus rhythmic patterns for the reel, jig, hornpipe and waltz. Features over 100 songs, and comes with a cassette that demonstrates several of the tunes. Reading music is not necessary.
00000097 Book/Cassette Pack....................$16.95

The Perfect Harmonica Method
by Jerry Perelman
Centerstream Publications
The harmonica opens a wonderful new avenue of musical adventure for classroom learning or individual playing. *The Perfect Harmonica Method* is the beginner's guide to learning to enjoy music and play the harmonica. It includes a Hohner harmonica and case, a demonstration cassette, and an easy-to-follow book. Developed by Jerry Perelman, this method has been proven over a period of years with thousands of successful students.
_____00000147..$15.95

- You'll like what you hear! -